# The Time
## *of*
# My Life

# The Time
## *of*
# My Life

## Patrick Swayze
## and Lisa Niemi

**ATRIA** PAPERBACK

*New York   London   Toronto   Sydney*

**ATRIA** PAPERBACK
A Division of Simon & Schuster, Inc.
1230 Avenue of the Americas
New York, NY 10020

First Atria Paperback edition July 2010

**ATRIA** PAPERBACK and colophon are trademarks of Simon & Schuster, Inc.

For information about special discounts for bulk purchases,
please contact Simon & Schuster Special Sales at
1-866-506-1949 or business@simonandschuster.com.

The Simon & Schuster Speakers Bureau can bring authors
to your live event. For more information or to book an event
contact the Simon & Schuster Speakers Bureau at
1-866-248-3049 or visit our website at www.simonspeakers.com.

Designed by Dana Sloan

Manufactured in the United States of America

10  9  8  7  6  5  4  3  2  1

Library of Congress Control Number: 2009029388

ISBN 978-1-4391-5858-6
ISBN 978-1-4391-5861-6 (pbk)
ISBN 978-1-4391-6591-1 (ebook)

*From Patrick:*
*For my dad, Jesse "Big Buddy" Swayze,*
*who taught me that a real man can be tough*
*and gentle at the same time*


*From Lisa:*
*For Patrick, who is more like his dad than he knows*

# The Time
*of*
# My Life

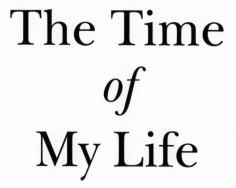

# Prologue

In late December 2007, life was looking pretty good. I had just wrapped shooting on the pilot of a new TV series, *The Beast*. My wife, Lisa, and I were enjoying a second honeymoon of sorts after a long, difficult period in which we had grown painfully apart. And I was feeling excited about new work, new directions, and the promise of the future.

Lisa and I were planning to spend New Year's Eve at our ranch in New Mexico, as we'd done for the past few years. But first, we stopped off in Aspen to visit a couple of friends. It was there that I got the first hint that something was wrong.

I had been having some digestive trouble, mostly acid reflux and a kind of bloated feeling, for a few weeks. I've had a sensitive stomach my whole life, so I hadn't thought much of it, but lately I just couldn't shake the constant discomfort. I wasn't hungry and felt sick whenever I did eat, but I'd always been pretty healthy, so I figured the feeling would pass eventually.

In Aspen, we all raised glasses of champagne for a toast. I took a sip, and as the champagne began to course through my esophagus to my stomach, I nearly choked—it burned like acid going down. It felt like I'd drunk lye, a sharp, searing pain that brought tears to my eyes. I'd never felt anything like it, but not wanting to ruin the festivities, I said nothing to Lisa. I was used to ignoring pain, so I just didn't drink any more champagne that night, and didn't think anything more about it.

Three weeks later, in January 2008, I learned that the burning in my stomach wasn't some minor irritation. It was the result of blockage in my bile ducts, which was caused by pancreatic cancer—just about the most deadly, untreatable cancer you can get.

When my doctor at Cedars-Sinai in Los Angeles said the words "pancreatic cancer," a single thought popped into my mind: I'm a dead man. That's what I had always thought when I heard someone had pancreatic cancer, and it usually turned out to be true. My doctor told me that my chances of surviving for more than a few months weren't high, and I had no reason to doubt him.

A lot of things go through your head when you get a death sentence handed to you, starting with *Why me? What did I do to deserve this?* Once the shock wears off, it's hard not to sink into bitterness, to feel that you've been singled out in a way that's not fair. For me, that initial shock quickly turned to self-criticism and blame. *Did I do this to myself? What could I have done differently? Is it my fault?*

In those first few weeks after my diagnosis, amid the whirlwind of figuring out treatments and medication, I struggled, with Lisa's help, to make sense of what was happening to me. Trying to counteract all the negative emotions that kept welling up—anger, bitterness, despair—I began thinking to myself, *I've had more lifetimes than any ten people put together, and it's been an amazing ride. So this is okay.*

I was trying to find a way to accept what was going on, but then a funny thing happened. I just couldn't. I wasn't ready to go, and I was damned if this disease was going to take me before I was good and ready. So I said to my doctor, "Show me where the enemy is, and I will fight him." I wanted to understand exactly what I was up against so I could go after this cancer rather than waiting for it to beat me. And in the year and a half since my diagnosis, that's exactly what I've done, with every ounce of energy I have.

Fighting cancer has been the most challenging and eye-opening experience I've ever had, and it has sent me on an emotional journey deeper than anything I've felt before. Facing your own mortality is the quickest way possible to find out what you're made of. It strips away all the bullshit and exposes every part of you—your strengths and weaknesses, your sense of self. Your soul.

It also leads you to confront life's hardest questions: Is there a heaven? Will I make it in? Has this life counted for something other than just my own narcissism? Have I lived a good life? Am I a good person? It's easy to dismiss these difficult questions when you have your whole life ahead of you. But when you're faced with your own mortality, they suddenly take on a whole new meaning.

There's a scene at the end of *Saving Private Ryan* that really resonated with me when I first saw it, and it does now more than ever. As an old man, Private Ryan muses aloud about whether he's lived a good life. "I tried to live my life the best I could," he says. "I hope that was enough." It's so hard to judge your own life, to know whether you've made a mark in this world. Doing this book was, in part, a quest to find that out for myself.

I've never been one to spend a lot of time dwelling in the past, so spending time with Lisa looking back at our lives has been really illuminating. Especially in light of what our future now holds, it has also been cathartic. I never felt like I had all the answers, and I certainly don't claim to now. Yet the one thing I realized as Lisa and I retraced the arc of our lives is that no matter what happened, we never, ever gave up—on each other, or on our dreams. I'm far from perfect, and I've made a lot of mistakes in my life. But that's one thing we both got right, and it's the one thing that's keeping me going today.

As I write this, sitting in our beautiful ranch home in New Mexico with the sun beaming down on the mountains, I realize yet again how much more I want to do in this life. Together with Lisa, I'll keep on pushing, keep on believing. Because that, in the end, is the greatest gift we have.

*Patrick Swayze*
*June 2009*

As Patrick and I have been writing this book, I couldn't help but be amazed by all the stories of things we've done and been through. It was surprising to me how hard we've both worked our whole lives, how focused and single-minded we could be. It must be the dancer in us. Always striving to be more, do better, never settle. And that drive to be better has served us well, particularly with all that we're going through now.

Looking back now, I wish I had done more of the proverbial "stop and smell the roses." So many gorgeous, beautiful things have happened in my life and I was too busy moving forward to really, truly recognize and enjoy them. I'm feeling different these days. Today I find myself much more willing to take luxurious, selfish pleasure in how beautiful a day is, the wonderful smell of my favorite mare's hair, and how much overflowing love I feel for my husband.

After Patrick was first diagnosed, I found myself wanting to go back in time and fix all the bumps that we had ever encountered. I wished we could start all over again so that this time we could do it differently. We could be wiser, avoid all those wrong turns we made, and not waste so much time. This time we would laugh more, touch each other more, and simply love each other in the way our true selves always have. And of course, if this daydream came true, I'd get a chance to live our lives together all over again, fulfilling my greatest wish—to have more time with him.

In some ways, getting to do this book gave me a passport into the past. But not in the way I had thought. It couldn't elongate my time with him, but it did show me that some of those bumps I wished I could get rid of don't look so bad when we keep coming out on the other side. And they're a testament to the strength of what we are together.

You'd think that when someone close to you receives a death sentence it would inspire amazing insights and lessons about life. I know that's what I thought. But after his diagnosis, and after I started to recover from feeling I was trapped in a perpetual nightmare, I looked around and couldn't see a damn lesson in sight. Yet slowly, as I've been dealing with getting past the initial grief and fear, living each day that comes and running around preparing for all the things one can't possibly prepare for, the lessons have started to ease out into the open. I couldn't force them out any sooner. They come in their own time when they, and you, are good and ready.

There's a lot of wisdom in the idea of living one day at a time. And when you might not have someone for long, that's what starts to happen.

I used to be afraid of time—that I'd run out of it, that I wouldn't have time to do all the things I wanted. Now I'm seeing each minute that passes as a victory. As something I'm proud of. It's like I can gather all these minutes into my arms as if they're an enormous mass of jewels. Look what I have—another moment! A kiss, a stroke of the skin on my husband's arm, the light coming through the window just so . . . Each of these jewels gives me the confidence to stand up and look Death in the face and say, "No one's going anywhere today."

I can help Patrick—I can coach him, love him, track his medications and calories, be there to kick him in the pants or just hold his hand if he needs it. But I can't save him. And I try to remember that. But I've got the best possible thing on my side: Patrick himself. I love that he's such a fighter. He's so amazingly strong and beautiful. He's my best weapon against this terrible disease.

You know, we were in New Mexico a couple of years after Patrick had broken both his legs in a life-threatening horse accident while filming *Letters from a Killer*. We walked out into the fresh mountain air, and he had taken off his shirt to enjoy the sun as we strolled into our beautiful fifty-acre pasture to visit with our five spirited Arabian horses. Patrick was rubbing one of the horses on her neck and I had walked off a ways for some reason or another. And I turned around just in time to see him grab a handful of mane and swing himself up on the mare's back. No saddle, no bridle, nothing.

She and the other horses started to trot off together and then, in a tight group, they launched into a full gallop, Patrick riding bareback in the middle of them through the open field. I couldn't believe it. I couldn't help but see how fantastic and free he looked. And I couldn't help but be pissed off. I mean, he'd just broken his legs a year or so earlier in that horse accident and he was going to risk doing it again?

The horses had their joyride and slowed to an easy trot, and Patrick hopped off blithely, unscathed. As he walked over to me he smiled a little sheepishly, waiting to see if I was going to admonish him. But I couldn't. I could only shake my head and try my best not to smile. This is the man who's taken on cancer. As always, he's on the ride of his life. And I know that he's going to ride this horse as far as it'll go.

*Lisa Niemi*
*July 2009*

# Chapter 1

Halloween night, 1970. It was a balmy Saturday evening in Houston when I ran onto the field with my Waltrip High School football teammates, ready for a big game with our crosstown rivals, the Yates Lions. We were pumped up to play, since we'd heard there would be college scouts in the stands checking us out. Little did I know then, but this night would change my life forever.

It was my senior year at Waltrip, and this was my chance to show the scouts what I could do. Yates was a good team, physical and aggressive, and the stands were packed with screaming fans, so the stage was set. At five-eleven and 180 pounds, I wasn't your typical big, bruiser football player, but I was fast, running the hundred-meter dash in just ten seconds. With those scouts in the stands, I was hoping to have a big game— we didn't have enough money for me to go to college, but a football scholarship would take care of that.

High school football isn't just a game in Texas; it's more like a religion. There's something magical about the smell of fresh-cut grass, the coaches yelling, the fans stamping their feet, and the twenty-two men on the field going at one another hand-to-

9

hand, in primal battle. I loved the competition, and the rough physicality of it. Whenever I took my position on the field, I had something to prove. I wanted to run faster, cut more sharply, and hit harder than anyone else out there.

But that night, I was the one who got hit hardest. On a midgame kickoff, I caught the ball and started to run. With blockers in front of me, I ran up one sideline, then cut back against the grain and tried to outrun the shifting defenders. But a couple of their big guys launched themselves at me, helmets first. One came in high, the other one low on my blind side. And they hit me at the exact moment my left leg planted on the ground.

My knee snapped, bending grotesquely, and I went down like a shot. In that moment, most of the ligaments in my knee had ripped in half, completely destroying the joint. But I didn't know that at the time, even as I screamed in pain hitting the turf. All I knew was that even though my knee felt like it had exploded, I wanted to get right up and walk it off—to show they hadn't hurt me, even though they had.

I tried to get up, but collapsed, as my left leg couldn't bear any weight at all. I got up again, determined to walk off that field, but again I fell to the grass. Finally, the coaches ambled over to check on me. One of them, a tough redneck son of a bitch, looked down at me and sneered, "Too much dancing, huh, Swayze?"—as if that, and not the two human rockets that had launched at me, had caused my injury. This was rough-and-tumble Texas, and even a star football player was the target of mockery if he happened to be a dancer, too. I glared through a haze of pain and said nothing as they finally lifted me up, put me on a stretcher, and carried me back to the locker room.

As I lay on a training table in the locker room, the pain in my knee began to dull, replaced by shock. And that was enough to make me want to keep playing. "Let me get back out there!" I told the trainer. "Let me just finish out the game!"

"Nope," the trainer said. "You're done."

But I wouldn't take no for an answer. "I swear, I'm okay," I told him. "Just let me walk it off and get back out there!" No matter how many times he shook his head, I wouldn't shut up—I just had to get back on that field.

"Okay, then," the trainer finally said, tired of hearing me jabber on. "Go ahead. Get up and go!"

I slid off the table, but as soon as my left foot touched the floor it felt like someone had jammed a dagger deep into my knee. It buckled, and I fell to the floor, passing out. The next thing I remember was hearing sirens and seeing the flashing lights of an ambulance.

My knee joint was pretty much destroyed, and I ended up having surgery—the first of many I'd have over the years. The doctors repaired as much damage as they could, after which I spent three months in a hip-to-toe cast, which left my leg completely atrophied and my knee joint hopelessly stiff.

For a young man who had always been athletic and active, being in a cast was difficult and painful, but it was nothing compared to the agonizing rehab process of physically breaking and loosening the scar tissue that had formed in the joint. My knee could barely bend. I remember lying in my bed at home, hearing my mother crying inconsolably in the next room. I thought I heard her say through her sobs, "His life is over. His life is over." It scared me. Would I be able to do all the things I'd done before the injury? Or would my physical abilities forever be compromised?

My days of playing football were over, but what would happen now to my dreams of competing in gymnastics, or dancing professionally? In all my eighteen years, I'd never questioned my ability to do anything I set my mind to do. But now, for the first time, I was facing a true test. Thanks to that one fleeting moment on a high school football field, it was the first of many I'd have to face.

My family's roots go way back in Texas, and my parents' relationship was the classic Texas story of the cowboy who falls in love with the city girl. Jesse Wayne Swayze, known to one and all as "Buddy," was a onetime rodeo champion who'd grown up on a ranch outside Wichita Falls. Unpretentious and bright, he worked for years as a butcher, then put himself through home study to get a degree in drafting. He got a job with an oil company and continued his studies, earning another degree and becoming a mechanical engineer. He put all the money he had into his family, especially into the dance company and school my mother ran.

My mom, Patsy Swayze, was a choreographer and teacher, and one of the founders of Houston's dance scene. She had the energy of a dancer combined with the steely strength and determination of a pit bull. Mom was an amazing teacher but a demanding one, and we kids worked hard to win her approval in a series of competitions we didn't yet realize we could never win.

I was the second of five kids, and the oldest boy. My older sister, Vicky, and I both studied dance with our mother from the time we could walk. Mom's studio, the Swayze Dance Studio, was like a second home for us, a place where we spent endless hours hanging out and studying dance. My mother never asked Vicky and me if we wanted to study dance—it was just expected of us. And not only that, but we were expected to be the absolute best at it. In fact, my mother chose the name Patrick for me because she thought "Patrick Swayze" would look good on a marquee. But like my dad, I went by the name "Buddy"—or, when he was around, "Little Buddy."

Our younger siblings, Donny, Sean, and Bambi, also felt the constant pressure to perform in whatever activities they undertook. We called it "growing up Swayze"—an almost manic drive to be the best, do the most, and lead the pack in whatever we attempted. Both our parents were very accomplished: Dad had been a Golden Gloves boxer and Mom was one of the leading lights of the Houston dance scene. But that's where the similarities between them ended.

My mother was a perfectionist, and she expected the same in her children, no matter what we did. This was a double-edged sword, as her pressure implanted in me a burning desire to be the best at everything, but it also led to a near-constant, deeply rooted feeling of inadequacy. I couldn't be everything she wanted me to be, for good reason—no one could. But I was going to do it or die trying, a trait that has never left me.

My dad was more laid-back, the gentle cowboy. He was the rock our family was built on, a steady and stable presence in our lives. In some ways, we were nurtured more by my father than by my mother, and growing up with a father who was both strong and sensitive made a huge impression on me. It made me realize that having a gentle side didn't make you less of a man. In fact, it made you a better one.

We didn't have a lot of money, especially while my dad was working in the butcher's shop, but my mother always carried herself with dignity. I can remember feeling embarrassed while walking into Mass one morning, since the sole of one of my shoes had partially torn off and made a flapping noise all the way down to my pew. I can also remember that our neighbors in North Houston kept their distance, since we were "those arts people"—not a label anyone really aspired to in 1960s Houston, Texas. Especially at that time, even Texas's big cities were still rough, redneck, conservative places—a fact I learned all too well as a young male dancer.

By junior high school, everybody knew I was a dancer, as I was always performing in theater productions and wore my hair long, unlike the other boys at school. I got picked on, called "fag," and beaten up more times than I can count, and each time it made me more determined to get those boys back, one way or another. But it wasn't until one particularly bad beating when I was about twelve that my dad finally stepped in and gave me the tools to do it.

Five boys had jumped me at once, and although I fought back with everything I had, those are bad odds for anyone—I got my butt handed to me. When I got home, with my face all bruised and cut, my dad decided it was time for me to learn hand-to-hand combat. My brother Donny and I had just started studying martial arts, since there was a Black Belt Academy in the shopping complex where Mom's studio was, but Dad had something else in mind. He'd been a serious boxer, and he wanted me to learn how to fight his way. So in addition to dancing, I spent the next couple of months studying martial arts and learning how to box.

When my dad thought I was ready, he drove me back up to the school. He walked me into the football coach's office and said, "I want you to pull those boys out of their classes so we can settle this thing." When Dad went on to say he wanted me to fight these kids again, Coach Callahan just stared at him. These bullies had kicked the shit out of me just a couple of months ago—and now my father wanted to invite them to go at me again? "But this time it isn't going to be five boys on one," my dad said. "It's gonna be one on one, fair and square."

It took some convincing, but times were different then, so Coach Callahan quickly deemed it acceptable educational policy to pull boys out of classes, put us in the weight shack by the football field, and let us fight it out. Dad and I walked down to the weight shack, and the coach soon met us there with the five boys. My dad was holding two pairs of boxing gloves, but when the first boy and I got ready to square off, he put them aside. "Just go ahead," he told us. "I don't think you need these."

"Now, hold on," the coach said. "We can't do this, Mr. Swayze." But though my dad was a gentle soul who rarely raised his voice, he did have a temper, which he unleashed at this moment. "Just go on ahead," he said to me, then turned back to the coach. "Buddy deserves a chance to do to these boys what they did to him," he said, his eyes burning with anger. "They think they're tough? We'll see how tough they are."

I won't deny that I was scared. My father obviously believed I was strong enough, and a good-enough fighter, to beat all five of these boys. As I prepared to square off against the first one, I could feel my adrenaline pumping—not because I was afraid of getting hurt, but because I didn't want to let my dad down. But I felt my senses sharpening and my heart beating faster, and I had a realization. I suddenly understood that you can conquer fear by making it work for you. And so I did. I beat all five of those boys that day, one by one. As each one left the weight shack, bloody and bruised, I could see the flickers of pride cross my dad's face.

That didn't solve my problems at school—in fact, once word got around that I was the new "tough guy," everybody wanted to fight me. And since I was playing violin at the time, the "tough guy" was an even more inviting target, with his ballet shoes stuck in his back pocket and a violin case in his hand. I got into plenty more scrapes with boys at school, but I never forgot the lesson of how to turn fear to my advantage—a lesson that has served me well my whole life.

And although my dad had taught me to fight, he also taught me two unbreakable rules about when and how to do it. "Buddy," he always said, "if I ever see you start a fight, I'll kick your ass. And if I ever see you not *finish* a fight, I'll kick your ass." If there's one thing I learned from my father, it's that you might not always win, but you never, ever give up. Ever since that day in the weight shack, I never have.

When I was about ten years old, I climbed onto the roof of a two-story house being built down the street. "Hey!" I yelled down to the construction workers below. "How much will you give me if I jump?"

The men looked up and saw a wiry kid, hands on his hips, perched at the edge of the roof. One of them shook his head. "You want us to give you money to jump off that roof and break your goddamn neck?" he yelled up at me.

"How much?" I asked. "Come on!"

"I'll give you twenty-five cents," the man replied, while the others chuckled.

"Give me fifty cents and I'll do it!" I yelled back.

He nodded and waved his hand. "Well, go on, then," he said.

And this was the moment I'd waited for. Everyone's eyes were on me, my blood started rushing, and I jumped off that roof—right into the sand pile they'd been using to mix the cement. I hit the pile and rolled, my momentum carrying me right back up to my feet after a couple of turns. The man reluctantly fished a couple of quarters out of his pocket and handed them to me.

I might have looked crazy to the men, but I'd spent my whole childhood running and jumping and flying through the air. I knew how to fall and how to roll, and as a result I careened around not afraid of anything. With all my gymnastics and dance lessons, I knew my body inside and out, and knew exactly what it was capable of.

As soon as my younger brother Donny was old enough to run with me, he and I charged through the woods near our house like a couple of daredevils. I always loved heroes like Doc Savage and Tarzan—not superheroes with special powers, but ordinary guys who pushed themselves to do extraordinary things. I'd play Tarzan and Donny would be Cheetah, or Boy, depending on the mood I was in. We'd swing around on a network of vines hanging from the trees behind our house, wearing our specially made Tarzan suits: old Speedo swimsuits with a belt around the waist and the crotch cut out to look like a loincloth. More than one neighborhood girl was shocked at catching sight of all the Swayze family jewels flying around overhead.

Doc Savage was a particular hero of mine because he was not only physically daring and brave, he was also a Renaissance man. He could do anything—he was an explorer, a scientist, an inventor, a martial arts expert, and a master of disguise. I wanted to be like Doc Savage, to be able to do absolutely everything. When I wasn't flying around, jumping off buildings and racing through the woods, I was up in our tree house with my chemistry set, trying to invent the perfect rocket.

The space race with the Russians was in full swing, and model rocketry was the latest and greatest hobby for boys in the sixties. I'd built and launched a few model rockets, but then decided to take it a step further and make my own fuel, too. I got my hands on some zinc dust and sulfur, and began mixing it up like a mad scientist. Unfortunately, I was about as careful as a thirteen-year-old boy knows how to be, which isn't nearly careful enough. I knocked my Bunsen burner right onto that mound of zinc and sulfur, and in about the time it took my eyes to get as big as saucers, I knew I had to get out of that tree house.

It took a few seconds for the mix to ignite, just enough time for me to fly out of the tree house door and tuck and roll to safety. The explosion was deafening, and as the tree house went up in flames I looked back at the smoke billowing out and thought, *Well, I'll just have to build another one.* I had no concept of the danger I'd put myself in, that I could have been hurt or even killed. Like most teenage boys, I felt invincible— a feeling that would continue well beyond my teenage years.

At the same time as I was being the wild man in the woods, I was continuing to study dance, gymnastics, and violin, and performing in musicals. I spent hours at Mom's studio, studying, sweating, and pushing to become the best male dancer Houston had ever seen. I loved the grace and strength of dance, and the sheer physical demands of it.

My mother saw that I had talent, and although she let me

mess around in the woods and hurl myself around with aban-
don, she did set some other rules to try to keep me safe. The
one I hated most was that she wouldn't let me have a motorcycle. She'd had two uncles in the police force who both died
in motorcycle accidents. So she was scared to death that I'd
wreck it and kill myself—either that, or I'd ride off and do
some drugs, drink some liquor, or get laid, like so many teenage boys in Texas.

"If I ever see you on a motorcycle," she'd tell me, "I'll chop
it up with an axe." My mother was strong and had a quick Irish
temper, and I'd felt the blow of her hand more than once. So
I knew she was capable of doing it.

But I wanted a motorcycle more than anything, so I decided
if she wouldn't let me have one, I'd make one myself. First, I
took an old bicycle frame, welded a plate on the bottom, and
put some fat tires on it. Next, I stole the engine off my dad's
lawn edger and mounted it on the bike frame. Once I got the
engine hooked up to the sprocket, I had myself a homemade
motorbike. It didn't go all that fast, which is maybe just as well
since the only brakes it had were my two boots pushing on the
front tire.

I'd tear around on that motorbike while Mom and Dad
were away, riding all over the neighborhood. As long as I got
the edger engine off and reassembled by the time they got
home, I was fine—but of course, one afternoon my mother
came home early, and I got caught. Just as she'd said, she went
after that motorbike with an axe, destroying not only the bike
frame but Dad's edger engine as well—putting me up shit
creek with both my parents, though I suspected Dad secretly
admired the ingenuity I'd shown. But that was the last motorcycle I had for a while.

•   •   •

All through junior high and high school, I continued to pursue all the things I loved doing: sports, music, dance, gymnastics, martial arts, sailing, skating, and diving. I also was a proud Boy Scout, rising to the rank of Eagle Scout while earning patches in everything I could get my hands on. Donny and I had gotten into throwing knives during our Tarzan phase, which started my lifelong fascination with nongunpowder weapons. In my determination to become Doc Savage, I wanted to try out—and master—every skill I possibly could.

I ran track, swam, and roller-skated competitively, and took up diving, which I did well in thanks to my gymnastics training. But the place where I could really earn the jocks' respect was on Waltrip's football team, where my speed and agility helped me excel in every aspect of the game—I played on offense, defense, and special teams, and was even named All-City Halfback. I didn't particularly like the locker-room culture of football, but I did love showing people what I could do on the field.

But with all that said, the number-one priority in our family was always the stage. Dancing, choreography, and teaching performance were my mother's life's work—and I was her golden boy, the son who would carry through on her dreams. Throughout my childhood, junior high, and high school years, I performed in summer stock musicals—*The Sound of Music, Gypsy, The Music Man*—always honing my ability to sing, dance, and act onstage. I pushed hard to be that perfect golden boy. And she always pushed back, urging me to try harder, do more, be better.

All the hard work paid off in my early teens, when I received scholarship offers to study with the Joffrey Ballet and the American Ballet Theatre in New York City. But I turned them down, deciding instead to continue to study with my mother and dance with the Houston Jazz Ballet Company, which she founded, and making myself available for the sports training that fell during the summer. At that point, I wasn't sure I wanted a life as a professional dancer. In fact, I was having real trouble figuring out what I wanted to do, with so many options to choose from. Gymnastics? Dancing? Sports? How could I possibly decide among them?

But then came that fateful Halloween night, and the injury that threatened to derail all those dreams. Lying in bed with a hip-to-toe cast after surgery on my knee, all I could think was, *Can I come back from this? Will I be able to do everything I could before?*

It wasn't long before I decided on the answer: Yes, I could, and I would—because I had to. Failure was simply not an option, so from that point on, I just refused to even let that thought enter my head. It didn't matter how hard I'd have to push, or how much pain I'd have to endure. I would will myself through it. This was the first time, but far from the last, that I would push myself through an impossible situation by force of will.

As soon as the cast came off, I began working out my leg again—lifting weights, stretching, running, balancing, anything I could do to get it back into shape. By now I was in my last semester of high school, and my next step depended on being back in fighting form. I had received a gymnastics scholarship to San Jacinto Junior College, about an hour's drive from Houston, and I was determined not to have to give it up.

I rehabbed my knee all spring and summer, and by September I was working out daily with the San Jacinto gymnastics team. It still hurt, and it swelled up quickly whenever I gave it a good workout, but soon I was back to doing everything I'd done before the injury. My goal was to compete in the Olympics, and my coach, Pat Yeager, told me I had a shot at it. He had coached the U.S. Women's Gymnastics Team and was a member of the Men's Olympic Gymnastics Committee, so he knew something about world-class gymnastics.

I couldn't have known it then, but the best thing about having gotten my knee back into shape wasn't going be the Olympics—or anything having to do with gymnastics, for that matter. It was the fact that once I'd gotten back into dancing shape, I could continue rehearsing and performing at my mom's studio, which had merged with the Houston Music Theater. So I was there when a particular fifteen-year-old girl with long blond hair started showing up.

# Chapter 2

I noticed Lisa Haapaniemi right away, with her lithe dancer's build, her long blond hair, and the look of indifference she had whenever she passed me by. Unlike the other girls, she usually acted like I wasn't even in the room and never looked me in the eye. So one day, when she walked by close enough, I decided it was time to get her attention. I reached down, pinched her rear end, and said, "Hey there, cutie!" She turned and glared at me like I'd just farted in church.

Now, in my defense, I'd grown up at the studio, and I'd been pinching and flirting with girls there ever since I was about three feet tall. But Lisa wasn't like the other girls. She knew who I was, and she'd been told I was something of a Casanova. She'd also heard that when I walked into a room, you had to raise the roof to let my head in, it was so big.

The truth was, I'd had a couple of girlfriends and liked to go out, but mostly I was just a flirt. I had never fallen in love, though I'd had my heart broken in that melodramatic way teenage boys do—most notably by an "older woman" named Dixie whom I'd seen kissing another guy when I was thirteen.

I had cried my eyes out then, vowing I'd never love another, when I had yet to learn the first thing about love.

Lisa was right that I was a showoff, but it all stemmed from an insecurity I didn't yet know I had. All I knew how to do was talk about things I accomplished. I was trying out for the junior Olympics gymnastics team! I was a stage star in Houston! I could run faster and punch harder than any guy in town! I never believed that people could like me for myself; I always felt I had to win them.

The second time I met Lisa, I tried to do just that—but it didn't have quite the effect I was looking for. I was auditioning for a musical we were doing at the Houston Music Theater, and when I noticed that Lisa was watching with a few other girls, I decided to ramp it up a notch. I sang the song with all the gusto I could, then ended with a spontaneous backflip. Lisa and the other girls just rolled their eyes.

Lisa was the opposite of me—quiet, introverted, and mysterious—and I'd never met anyone like her. In Houston in the seventies, you were either a surfer, a doper, or a goat roper—a cowboy. Lisa had a reputation for being a doper, and although she did occasionally smoke pot, her reputation stemmed partly from the fact that people didn't know what to make of her. Most girls in Houston weren't quiet and self-contained—they had big hair and personalities to match. Lisa came from a Finnish family, a cool, blond, self-confident bunch that included five brothers, none of whom would be thrilled if the "Casanova" Buddy Swayze tried to move in on their little sister.

In the fall of 1971 I started San Jacinto Junior College on my gymnastics scholarship, but was still living at home, driving the thirty or so miles to campus each day. When I wasn't in classes or practicing with the gymnastics team, I was either at my mom's studio or managing the ice rink at the Houston Galleria. I had grown up roller-skating competitively and loved honing my ice skating skills, and I even started working on a pairs routine with my skating partner, Caroline. But there was another reason I liked working at the ice rink: I'd sometimes catch sight of Lisa hanging out at the mall.

I'd see her coming and going with her friends, occasionally going off with some guy to smoke in the parking lot or jump into his car and drive around. Although she was as blond and pretty as a cheerleader, she had the air of a "bad girl" about her, mostly because she seemed so hard to get to know.

But when Lisa started her freshman year at the High School for Performing and Visual Arts, she discovered dancing. At first, she wasn't as interested in dancing as she was in theater— she signed up for classes only because she had to declare a secondary course of study at HSPVA. But to her surprise, she fell in love with it, and by the spring of her freshman year, she'd made up her mind to become a professional dancer. She took a job at the Parfumery, located at the opposite end of the ice rink, to raise money to move to New York—so instead of seeing her hanging around smoking, now I'd see her going to and from work, a new sense of purpose on her face. And occasionally I'd "casually" wander down to talk to her and just check out what was going on.

I still had my dream, too—of making the Olympic gymnastics team—and I trained long hours at San Jacinto to make it happen. But that dream came to a crashing halt during my freshman year, when all the sweat, tears, and effort of getting my knee into shape after the football injury came undone in a single moment.

It happened at a competition, as I was warming up on the rings. This was my strongest event, all the more so because I didn't have to worry about my knee on anything but the dismount—success on the rings depended almost entirely on the strength of my arms and torso.

During competitions, some of the other guys warmed up extensively, doing practically their whole routines in preparation. But I liked to gain a little psychological edge by simply strolling up to the rings, executing a single move perfectly, and then strolling confidently off the mat. This was my usual warm-up, and I loved that moment of knowing my competitors were watching me walk off, not a care in the world, after nailing one perfect move.

I walked up to the lower rings and pulled myself into an inverted position, my body rigid and toes pointed. Concentrating on having perfect poise, I forgot for a split second that I was on the lower rings, not the higher ones, which hung a few feet higher in the air. So after showing off this one move, when I began my dismount I thought there was more room than there actually was between me and the floor. I executed a perfect dismount for the high rings, spinning into a somersault—but then I crashed hard to the mat, jamming both legs into the ground.

Blinding pain shot through my body, and I knew I'd injured the same knee again. It was agony to lie on the mat, knowing I'd hurt myself—and knowing it was because of a stupid mistake.

For the second time in two years, I was faced with surgery, a cast, and rehab. Some days I was so frustrated the tears just took over. I couldn't stand to be unable to run, to jump, to dance. And I couldn't stand the uncertainty about whether I'd be able to do so again. So, as I'd done the first time, I just made up my mind again that no matter what and no matter how hard it would be, I would get myself back into dance shape.

I continued at San Jacinto, and the more time I spent away from home, the more I began to realize that there was a whole big world out there waiting to be explored. Even if I couldn't be an Olympic gymnast, there were still a million other things out there that interested me. Yes, gymnastics had been my dream—and it stung like hell to know I'd missed my chance to achieve it. But I somehow knew instinctively that when one dream dies, you have to move on to a new one. The unhappiest people in this world are those who can't recover from losing a dream—whose lives cease to have meaning. I wasn't going to let that happen to me. It was a revelation that would later save my life.

Once again, I faced the question: What did I want to be? Who was Patrick Swayze, and what did he have to offer the world? I still wanted so much—to dance, to ice-skate, to sing, to act. I also wanted to become a pilot, and I learned that if I finished two years at San Jacinto, getting my associate arts degree in aviation, I could go into the military and hope to get into flight school. For a while, that's what I decided I would do, even though the Vietnam War was raging on the other side of the world, sucking young men like me into its jungles and sending them home changed—if it sent them home at all.

But before long, I realized the performing bug was just too strong for me to consider doing anything else. I rehabbed my knee again and kept working out at Mom's studio, building my strength and flexibility with the goal of performing again. And of course, being at the studio meant I would see Lisa, who was in my thoughts more and more.

I was still intrigued by this mysterious, beautiful girl, but she acted as cool as ever to me. But then came the moment we first danced together onstage. And suddenly, everything changed.

We were performing an exhibition of classical dance at a junior high school auditorium in 1972. Lisa and I had learned and rehearsed the pas de deux from the ballet *Raymonda.* Just before we stepped out onstage, I kissed her on the cheek for good luck, but that wasn't the magic moment. The magic happened when she took my hand to start dancing, and our eyes locked.

It felt like an electric charge suddenly coursed through my body. I looked into Lisa's eyes, and it was as if I was seeing her for the first time. We moved together as one, and I felt a stirring deep in my soul. It was a fleeting moment, but I never forgot it. But after the dance was done, I didn't mention it to her, afraid that the feelings had been mine alone.

Not long after that, we were paired up in yet another dance—one that threatened to make it embarrassingly clear how I felt about her. We were at my mom's studio, rehearsing a more avant-garde dance with some pretty provocative moves. At one point, I was supposed to ease Lisa down onto the floor and then lie on top of her. Well, you can imagine the effect this had on me, a healthy twenty-year-old guy wearing tights.

The dance called for us to lie like that for a long, long while. I felt shy and could never look her in the eye, but it was the first time I really got to smell her. And she smelled *good.* When it was time to move away, I was afraid that someone might note my "primal stirrings," and quickly turned away to stretch and adjust my legwarmers. Needless to say, I couldn't wait for the next rehearsal.

Now it was clear that I really liked her, so I went ahead and asked her out on a date. But when you start to like someone who used to be a friend, you get shy—and that's how I felt. I suddenly didn't know what to do with myself when I was around her. Fortunately, she did agree to go out on a few dates with me, but they were hardly the stuff of great romance.

First, I'd show up at her house, and one of her five tall, steely Nordic brothers would answer the door. He'd give me the third degree—Where was I taking Lisa? What time would I bring her home?—before she finally came out and we could get out of there. Then, we'd go to dinner and have awkward conversations, which basically consisted of me telling her about how great I was and her seeming utterly unimpressed. I just didn't have any idea how to talk to a girl—or anyone, for that matter. But I knew I liked her, and I wanted her to like me. I just didn't have any idea how to make that happen.

As my time at San Jacinto drew to a close, it looked as if I might not even get a chance to try. As I was mulling over what my next step might be, I got invitations to join the Ice Follies, Holiday on Ice, and Disney on Parade traveling shows. I loved ice skating, and joining one of the ice shows would mean pairing up with an excellent partner, Rulanna Rolen. But I loved dancing—and the idea of playing Prince Charming—even more. So despite lingering knee troubles, I signed up to join the Disney on Parade traveling company as it toured all over the United States, Canada, and Latin America. It was time to see the world.

Disney on Parade was a huge traveling show, with dozens of dancers and a giant stage set. We would perform in arenas and coliseums, with billowing blue lamé curtains, a full-scale castle with towers, and a huge egg-shaped screen projecting the stories of *Snow White, Fantasia,* and other Disney classics. I was excited to have my first performing job outside Houston—and excited to be traveling to places I'd only read about in books.

The dancers made $125 a week, which felt like a lot of money, especially since we all doubled, tripled, and quadrupled up in our living arrangements on the road. Most of the dancers were women, and of the few who were men, even fewer were straight men. So the opportunities for me in terms of finding women to date were just about endless.

Unfortunately, I still didn't know how to communicate with women, or anybody else. I just sounded like an egotistical ass whenever I talked, as I couldn't stop going on and on about myself. For one thing, my knee kept blowing up after each performance, the joint swelling painfully due to the rigors of the show. One dance in particular—the Russian Cossack dance, where you do repeated deep pliés with arms folded and legs flying—caused me no end of trouble. It got so bad that I had to go to the hospital in every city to get the fluid drained from my knee. And the more knee trouble I had, the more I had to talk about it.

But after I had initially alienated just about everyone with my incessant blathering, people started realizing that I wasn't really egotistical, just insecure. And after a while, they started to accept and even befriend me. I ended up making a ton of friends during Disney on Parade and began to understand that I didn't have to win everybody all the time—that in fact, trying to win people only drove them away. Like a puppy learning not to chew on things, I trained myself not to talk about myself all the time.

I began dating one woman who was in the show, a good-looking blonde who had a party-queen reputation. She was a wild one, the kind of girl who liked trouble, and at first I was drawn to her dangerous air. Part of me just wanted to see if I could win her, but once I did, I realized she wasn't at all the kind of woman I was looking for. It sounds corny, but I really did believe in Snow White and Prince Charming—I wanted to find a woman whom I could ride off into the sunset and share my life with. I'm not sure I was even aware of it at the time, but subconsciously I was comparing all the women I met to Lisa.

Meanwhile, Lisa was back in Houston having problems of her own. She'd been having a lot of trouble sleeping, and her insomnia eventually got so bad she had to drop out of high school. She'd always had trouble fitting in, and now, with the onset of a creeping depression, she felt even more alienated. This was the beginning of what she later called her "blue period."

Things at home were tough, too—her parents had a very contentious relationship, and their dynamic affected the entire family. Eventually, Lisa began lying awake at night in fear. Her house didn't feel like a safe place emotionally, and she began to feel an overpowering sense that if she walked out the door of her bedroom in the middle of the night, she'd be eaten by wolves. It wasn't a rational fear, but this was a scary time for a teenage girl who had come to feel that no place was safe for her. Finally, she decided that she had to get out of her parents' house, at least until things cooled down a bit. So one day at the studio, she asked my mom if she could come stay at our house for a while.

My mother, who could be so hard on her own kids, had come to adore Lisa. For one thing, Lisa had started dancing incredibly late—no serious female dancer starts in her teens, as Lisa had. But Lisa was so determined, and so gifted, that my mother invested all her teaching skills and all the nurturing she could muster to help her out. Lisa had experienced a life-changing moment at age fifteen when she made a conscious decision to pursue dancing seriously. She'd stopped smoking dope and began working out at my mom's studio seven days a week—she even got the key from my mom so she could work out when nobody was there.

Lisa's dedication thrilled my mother, who in return was a mentor to her, providing validation and emotional support. So when Lisa asked if she could move into the Swayze house for a couple of weeks, my mom didn't hesitate at all before saying yes.

Lisa stayed at our house for a couple of weeks, and as it happened, I was home for much of that time. Early on, before my mother really knew Lisa, my mom had told me, "Buddy, I don't want you dating Lisa. She's bad news." But then my mother had watched Lisa transform herself into a serious dancer, and now she had a slightly different message. "Buddy," she said. "I don't want you dating Lisa. I don't want you messing her up."

My mom didn't know it, but the attraction between Lisa and me had been growing for some time. She had seemed indifferent to me all those months, but it turned out she was interested in me, too—she was just shy, and acting like she didn't care was her way of covering it up. But during those two weeks when Lisa stayed with us, she and I took every opportunity to steal time together. When Mom was in the kitchen, we'd be behind the swinging door in the dining room, making out. After everyone in the house had gone to sleep, we'd sneak out to the living room and fool around on the couch. We still weren't technically "dating," but man, we couldn't get enough of each other.

In fact, I had been seeing other girls—and the very day Lisa came to stay at our house I had a date with a girl named Mimi, which led to an uncomfortable moment. Vicky Edwards, the daughter of Louisiana governor Edwin Edwards, had gone out of town and loaned me her Corvette. With such a hot car at my disposal, I'd asked Mimi out for that Saturday night, to go to the Houston Rodeo. But when Lisa moved into our house that afternoon, Mom expected me to give her a ride to the rodeo, too.

The Corvette was a two-seater, of course, so Lisa took the front seat and Mimi squeezed between us, sitting on the tiny console. Mimi was a nice-enough girl, but she was pretty much the embodiment of what Lisa and I had joked about privately— the big-haired, heavily made-up Houston girl. To my embarrassment, Mimi kept tickling my ear and kissing me all the way to the rodeo, as Lisa sat silently. I felt ridiculous and embarrassed, yet even though it was clear to anyone paying attention that Lisa was the only girl I truly cared about impressing, I still didn't understand what she meant to me.

When my time with Disney on Parade ended, it was time to figure out my next step. After all the rigors of the show, my knee was pretty wrecked, and I looked forward to having some time to heal. But fate intervened when I received a scholarship to study with the Harkness Ballet in New York City.

Touring with Disney on Parade had made me realize how deeply dance was rooted in my soul. Of all the things I loved to do, nothing came close to the feeling dancing gave me—a feeling of complete emotional and physical freedom, as if your spirit is soaring in all directions at once. It's hard to capture in words the sheer joy and fulfillment that the act of dancing can bring. All I knew was, I wanted to do it forever. And Harkness was my chance to do it professionally, at the highest level.

My mother, who had pushed me and pushed me as a young dancer, didn't want me to accept the scholarship. She knew that ballet dancing is just about the hardest thing you can put a knee joint through, and a company like Harkness was guaranteed to push me to my absolute limit. My mother didn't want to see me go through that—but also, true to form, she didn't want me to attempt something that she felt I couldn't be the best at.

Of course, if there's one sure way to get Patrick Swayze to do something, it's to tell me I can't do it. You don't think I can dance with one of the greatest professional ballet companies in the world? Watch me.

So I packed up a couple of suitcases and got ready for the move to New York. This was it—Buddy Swayze was heading for the bright lights and the big city! I was excited at the chance to test my stuff against the best dancers in the business. And I knew exactly whom I wanted to spend my last evening in Houston with: Lisa.

I invited her to dinner at St. Michel's, a fancy French restaurant in town. We ate escargot and talked for what must have been hours. Lisa and I had gotten more and more comfortable with each other, and we talked easily about dancing, life, and the future that stretched enticingly ahead of us. At the end of dinner, she gave me a fifty-cent piece. "This is for luck," she said, pressing it into my hand. In return, I gave her a broken Mickey Mouse watch I'd gotten during Disney on Parade.

I didn't realize yet that I was falling in love with Lisa, but I did know she was the kind of person I always wanted to have in my life. I gave her a card that night that she's kept all these years. It gives a pretty good idea of how I was feeling about her:

*Lisa, I really can't tell you how much you've come to mean to me in such a short time, as a friend, and as someone I could really care for. Remember the happiness we shared and I hope in your mind you know that I don't want what we shared to end! I'll miss you very much and will think of you often. Work hard at your dancing and I'll do the same, and maybe, someday . . . !*
*My heart be united with yours,*
*Buddy*

It was a magical night—or at least, it was until I dropped Lisa off at her house and was driving home. As I was making my way through the suburb of Bellaire, I looked in my rearview mirror to see police lights flashing. My stomach fell. Earlier that day, I'd realized the license plates on my car were out of date, so I'd taken the plates off my dad's truck and put them on my car. The police were pulling me over because they'd run a check and discovered the plates were on the wrong vehicle.

The police in Bellaire had a reputation for being nasty and aggressive, and they certainly lived up to it that night. After they pulled me over, I tried to explain why I'd switched the plates, but the officers weren't having any of it. They pinned me hard up against a chain-link fence, frisked me, and put me in the back of their car to take me down to the precinct. I was under arrest.

I spent half the night in jail, until my dad was able to come down to bail me out. He didn't have enough cash on him to do it, though, and there were no ATMs then. So I fished around in my pockets and gave the police the rest of my cash, too—including the lucky coin from Lisa.

Getting arrested and thrown into a jail cell certainly wasn't the big send-off I'd hoped for. But at least the next day I was on my way, with fingers crossed that my luck in New York would be better than my luck on my last night in Houston.

# Chapter 3

My first apartment in New York City was at 45 West Seventieth Street. Unlike the clean, upscale neighborhood of today, the Seventies then were still rough around the edges. My street was at least decent, and affordable, and it had the bonus of being close to Central Park. But the apartment itself turned out to be less pleasant than the surroundings.

I was moving into a basement apartment with a fellow Harkness dancer, and as I descended below sidewalk level, I realized it wasn't going to be pretty down there. The lack of natural light was depressing enough, but it wasn't nearly as bad as the rat droppings, the musty smell, and the water stains on the walls. My family didn't exactly live in a mansion in Houston, but I could hardly believe this was the place I'd now be calling home—it was a hovel. At a Harkness trainee stipend of just forty-five dollars a week, though, it was all I could afford, even working extra jobs in my spare time.

I was scared to death about how my knee would hold up at Harkness. Part of me knew it was crazy even to have accepted the scholarship, but I wasn't going to let that stop me. I've made a huge amount of headway in my life trading on the invincibility of youth: Whether I was truly invincible or not, I operated as if I were, and to a certain extent believed that I was. This would be no different—I would just dance and suffer and grit my teeth whenever it hurt. And it would be worth all the pain when I made the leap from trainee to company member.

For all the fear I felt about my knee, I should have been equally afraid of the infamous Harkness regimen. In addition to the physical stress of dancing in up to six classes a day, torquing and twisting your joints and pushing your endurance to the limit, Harkness also put some of its dancers on a special diet aimed at virtually eliminating body fat. The Harkness diet allowed dancers to consume just five hundred calories a day— basically, lettuce and a few bites of turkey, plus vitamin shots.

And that wasn't all. The Harkness doctors also came up with a shot that was supposedly made from the extract of a pregnant woman's urine. This extract was said to encourage your body to live off its own fat tissue, so even those who had almost no body fat to begin with still dropped pounds, as the small deposits of fat between muscles melted away. I had always been lean, through constant training, but my arms and shoulders were big—I looked like Godzilla compared to the other male dancers. But under the Harkness regimen, I transformed my body. I dropped fifteen pounds and developed the streamlined physique of a dancer.

The women in Harkness had it even rougher. At this point, nobody had written an exposé like Gelsey Kirkland's 1996 book *Dancing on My Grave,* which detailed the dark side of the professional ballet world. Gelsey was dancing with the New York City Ballet and American Ballet Theatre at the same time I was at Harkness, and I often partnered her at pas de deux class. The tales she told in her book of the rampant eating disorders, drug use, and emotional trauma that dancers faced matched what I saw during those years.

Female bodies aren't really supposed to look like the bodies of ballet dancers, who are prized for their slender hips and prepubescent figures. So no matter how thin a dancer was, she was always encouraged to lose more by the Harkness tribunal, which kept tabs on dancers' progress. "Lose five more pounds" was the mantra, even if the women had already shed pounds on intensive, crazy diets. The pressure was so bad that two women even died during my time at the ballet. They just pushed themselves farther than their emaciated bodies could handle.

Everything my mother had said was true—the amount of suffering you had to undergo to become a professional ballet dancer was overwhelming. I stuck to it, dancing and dieting to prove that I was ready to take my spot in the company. But the one thing I couldn't control, of course, was my knee. And with the daily abuse of dancing, it got worse than ever.

As had happened during my days touring with Disney on Parade, my knee began swelling up like a balloon after I danced. I would always ice it to bring the swelling down, but at other times there was just too much fluid in the joint and I'd have to get it drained. This was an unpleasant procedure—I'd go to one of the company orthopedists who worked with Harkness, and he would insert a long needle into my knee to let the fluid out. There were times when the joint was so inflamed, I'd watch it swell right back up just after having it drained. Then I had no choice but to go home, ice it some more, and just hope it would be ready for class the next day. Yet even if it wasn't, it didn't matter. I'd have to dance anyway.

At one point, I felt a strange burning sensation I'd never had before, as if my knee was on fire inside. The joint swelled up worse than ever, and I began to worry that something was seriously wrong. I was taking antibiotics—some weeks I had to choose between them and food, as I didn't always have enough money for both—but this felt like an infection. As it turned out, it was a fast-moving staph infection that ended up threatening more than just my dancing career.

When I went to the doctor to get it checked out, he told me I needed to stay overnight in the hospital for treatment. I told him that was impossible—I had too much to do. I couldn't miss any classes, and I didn't want anyone to think my knee wasn't strong enough for the rigors of dancing.

The doctor looked at me with a grave expression. "Patrick," he said, "this is a serious staph infection. If we don't nip it in the bud, you could lose your leg."

I stared at him, stunned into silence. I had been pushing myself so hard, it had never occurred to me that I could actually be putting my health in danger. Ever since I'd hurt my knee in that football game, I had forced myself to operate as if it was fine, as there was no other way to do all the things I wanted to. The doctor's words scared me, but I knew that after I got it treated, I'd have to push on as before. I'd have to find a way.

If it hadn't been for my knee trouble, I would have made the Harkness company already. Even though I had lost some weight and muscle mass, I was still a rarity in the world of ballet, a male dancer who actually looked like a man onstage. Most male dancers were slender and graceful, amazing dancers—but they didn't look like what the ballet companies wanted. I knew that on the most fundamental level, the purpose of the male dancer was to make the woman look beautiful, and my performances were geared toward exactly that. I aimed to look strong and masculine, and to present the female dancer in the best light I could.

I was a good partner, and a good soloist, which is a rare combination in the ballet world. For that reason, I was a sought-after dancer—which of course made me all the more reluctant to give up.

Amid all this dancing, dieting, and worrying, I had to find ways to bring in more money. The stipend wasn't enough for anyone to live on, so despite the fact that we were often exhausted from workouts and rehearsals, many of the dancers worked extra jobs to pay the rent.

I worked for a time at a Hallmark card store, and also lifeguarded at a subterranean men's health club near my apartment. I sang and played guitar in the clubs down in Greenwich Village, which was a hotbed of creative energy, with artists on every corner and an exciting vibe. New York in the 1970s was very different from the New York of today—it was rough, a little wild, with an anything-goes feel to it. Energy seemed to pulsate through the streets, and being young there made you feel as if you could do anything. And that anything could happen.

The next job I got was a perfect example of that. In early September 1973, I got word that the Harkness Ballet's benefactor, the oil heiress Rebekah Harkness, had specifically requested me for a rather unusual assignment.

Mrs. Harkness had commissioned Spanish artist Enrique Senis-Oliver to paint a gigantic mural for the brand-new Harkness Theater then being built at Lincoln Center. Called *Homage to Terpsichore,* the painting stretched from the stage to the very top of the proscenium and down both sides, and consisted mostly of what *Time* magazine would later call "an agonized, thrusting morass of naked dancers."

Well, those naked dancers were all me. Over a period of several weeks, I posed and flexed so Enrique could paint my nude form over and over in the mural. Enrique and I spent many exhausting hours perched on scaffolding thirty feet off the ground in the freezing theater while he painted the ceiling. As a thank-you he painted my face on the mural's centerpiece—a towering twenty-foot-high portrait of me leaping naked toward the sun, with a cape of peacock feathers trailing behind me.

As a letter I wrote to Lisa right when I got that modeling gig shows, the fall of 1973 was a very good time for me in New York. I'd just returned after seeing her in Houston, and I was filled with the excitement of being young, in the city, and having my whole life ahead of me:

*Well, Lisa,*

*I'm back! I was really dreading coming back while I was on the plane, but now that I'm back, it's great! Everything is fine, my rent is paid, and everything is well at Harkness.*

*My first day was fabulous, I saw all my friends and had great classes. Plus Mrs. Harkness called the "House" and said she wanted me to do the modeling for the men's bodies to be painted in the new theater! And they're going to do a 20' portrait of me! Mrs. Hynes told me today, and it totally freaked me out! So I'm getting $25.00 per hour for modeling. Also the*

*artist wants me to do some modeling for portraits and some*
*shows coming up! And I've got an audition for that club*
*(singing) tomorrow. . . .*

*I went walking tonight after modeling, and the street was*
*bustling, and the fountain at Lincoln Center was so neat, and*
*everything seems to be going my way, that I just started run-*
*ning and singing! People thought I was crazy but I didn't*
*care! . . .*

*Well, I've got tons of work ahead of me but I'm looking*
*forward to it so much. There is hardly anyone in class because*
*of the summer students being gone, and it's really fine! You*
*know, I didn't leave sad Wednesday, I really felt good; that is*
*about you. I know if we are meant to be, that we'll get it*
*together one day. Over such a short time, you've grown to mean*
*a lot to me, I want to always be great friends. Work hard and*
*maybe you'll be up here before you know it!*

*I miss you much and hope it's the same. Tell everyone*
*"Hello" and I miss 'em, okay? Stay happy, and write!*
*Missingly yours,*
*Buddy*

My feelings for Lisa were growing, but I was still scared to
admit it outright—either to her or to myself. I was hoping
against hope that she'd get a ballet scholarship, too, and come
up to New York City. But at the same time, I hedged my bets by
continuing to see other women, most notably a fellow Harkness dancer named Deleah.

Just a month after sending the letter above, I sent Lisa another one, dated October 16, 1973, in which I told her about
Deleah.

*Lisa, I think I have found someone I care for, a lot. Her name is Deleah Shafer. We started out incredible friends, and have steadily grown closer. She is on tour with the company now, so it gets kind of lonely sometimes. Lisa, I really hope this isn't just a passing fancy, because I feel so much love in me now, that I need someone to give it to. I guess the only thing to do is wait and see.*

I did like Deleah very much, but deep down I think I was hoping to make Lisa jealous. The rest of the letter is all about how I was dropping Lisa's name at Harkness, trying to help her secure a scholarship—and I even offered to have her stay at my apartment whenever she did make it up to New York. "It will save quite a bit of money, if it would be cool on the 'home front,' " I wrote, presumably with a straight face. I knew Lisa's parents wouldn't approve of her living with me in New York, but I wanted to plant that seed anyway.

After sending that letter, I even called Lisa for advice on dating Deleah, though it was probably really an attempt to find out how she felt about it. Despite the intensity of the feelings Lisa and I obviously had for each other, we both were trying very hard to protect ourselves. We both came to the relationship feeling like, "I don't want this person to get to me"—we were afraid of being too vulnerable, afraid of getting hurt. So both Lisa and I made a big show of just wanting to be friends, at least until the other person made the first move.

If I hoped to make Lisa jealous, though, I obviously didn't know her very well. In fact, she had a completely different response—but one that was ultimately far better than jealousy. As she later told me, she came to a turning point of sorts after I called her for advice about Deleah. She realized that more than anything, she wanted me to be happy. The way she saw it, her feelings for me ran deeper than simply wanting to lay claim to me or own my attentions. She began to see me in a different light—as someone she cared really deeply for, rather than someone she just liked messing around and talking with.

Of course, I didn't know any of this—I just knew that Lisa had reacted coolly to the notion that I had a new girlfriend. We kept writing back and forth and talking on the phone, though, so our relationship continued to grow even if we didn't quite know where it was going. And it probably would have continued that way, except that in 1974, Lisa finally got her scholarship to Harkness. She was coming to New York City, and despite her mother's hope that she'd move into the Barbizon Hotel for Women, she'd decided to take me up on my offer to live with me at my new place on West Seventy-fourth Street.

Lisa moved to New York in the summer of 1974, and I threw out a few people who'd been staying at my place, so it would just be the two of us. I wasn't exactly sure what the situation between us would be, but I wanted to make sure we had the space to explore it without six other roommates getting in the way.

As I soon discovered, Lisa had very distinct ideas about what we'd be doing together—and not doing. Despite the fact that we'd had plenty of makeout sessions in Houston over the years, she made it clear we'd be living together as roommates, not as lovers. Lisa, who was now eighteen, had been dancing seriously for three years and she was absolutely driven to do one thing: make it as a dancer. Now that she'd made it to New York, she didn't want any distractions getting in her way.

I wanted to make the Harkness company, too, of course, and I was incredibly focused on that goal. But my feelings for Lisa grew stronger and stronger the more time we spent together. After just a few weeks, I had no doubt that Lisa was the woman I wanted to be with. She was deep, talented, driven—and beautiful. As I played one of my favorite records of that summer—*The Best of Bread*—Lisa would catch sight of me gazing at her whenever the song "Baby I'm-a Want You" came on. She knew what I was feeling, and it frightened her.

But the attraction between us was so strong, and the intensity of our emotions so high, that something eventually had to give. And boy, did it. When Lisa and I finally got together in the winter of 1974–75, a few months after she'd moved in with me, it was like the dam had broken and the flood came rushing in. With all the fooling around we'd done in Houston, we'd never had sex together, but once we did—well, suffice it to say I'd never felt such passion in my life, and I couldn't get enough of it. We were intoxicated by each other, and when we weren't dancing or working, we were most often at our apartment spending every hour we could together.

We'd stay up all night, talking, laughing, and just enjoying each other. The intensity of it was thrilling—I never thought I could feel so strongly about another person. We were discovering so much about each other, and learning about ourselves, too, all in the excitement of first love.

Lisa felt it, too, but she was also scared. She worried about giving in to her feelings for me when she wanted to be totally focused on dancing. And she wondered whether she was making a mistake by getting so deeply involved with me.

Years later, Lisa dug up her diary pages from that time, and
they show how deeply torn she was over what was happening
between us.

I really don't know what to do (concerning Buddy). I'm
so frightened. I want to sit down and talk it over with
him, but I'm afraid I might startle him too much or him
think I'm jumping to conclusions. . . .

Sometimes I wonder whether I'm being shallow and
just getting carried off like so many girls I know always
do. God, I'm so afraid. I've never done anything like this
before and I feel danger in getting close to a person and
caring more than I should. . . .

I wonder if I should move out. I might have to. But I'd
see him every day anyway [at Harkness] so there's not
much good for my head in that. What I should do is find
a way to get out and away as often as possible. I can't get
my life too tied to his.

I had no idea Lisa was considering moving out, which was
no doubt a good thing, as it would have scared me to death.
Looking back, these are the musings of a young woman who's
feeling torn in different directions and afraid to make a wrong
step. But I wouldn't have seen it that way. I'd have felt that she
was rejecting me, which would have rocked my fragile self-
esteem to the core. My feelings for her were now so strong,
and I was so sure of them, that I felt paralyzed at the idea that
I might lose her.

I wanted to feel the way we were feeling forever, to lock in
this relationship and this love. Lisa and I had talked a little bit
about where our relationship was headed, but I never got the

sense that she was anxious to commit to anything long-term. But I was. I wanted to marry Lisa. And one night in the spring of 1975, as we were playing around on the couch, I decided it was time to raise the subject.

We were wrestling and tickling each other, just messing around, and all of a sudden I said, "Lisa, why don't we get married? Why don't we just go ahead and do it?"

Of all the responses a man hopes to hear to this question, dead silence isn't one of them. But Lisa was quiet for a moment before responding slowly. "Yeah, sure," she said. "That could happen."

I sat up, every nerve ending on alert. "When do you want to do it?" I asked her.

"Well," she said, pondering, "how about fall of next year?" Meaning, the fall of 1976—nearly a year and a half away.

I could feel panic rising from my chest to my throat. For some reason, I just knew that unless we got married right away, it was never going to happen and I would lose Lisa forever. "No," I said. "If we're going to do it, let's do it right away—like, next month."

Now it was Lisa's turn to panic. All the fears she already felt, of suppressing her own desires in order to be with me, of getting distracted from her dancing, were coming to a head right now. She was eighteen years old, and although she loved me, she didn't feel ready to get married. But she knew me well enough to know how sensitive I was, and how hurt I'd feel if she turned me down outright. So she had tried to buy herself some time—but I wasn't having it.

"Lisa, we need to get married right away," I told her. And that was that—I wouldn't take no for an answer. I told her I loved her and needed her, and couldn't live without her. I even told her that if she wouldn't marry me now, I'd run my motorcycle into a stop sign. I'm not proud of that particular moment, but it's evidence of just how afraid I was to lose her. No matter how confidently I projected myself onstage and in everyday life, inside I was still a scared boy—afraid of rejection and willing to do whatever was necessary to stave it off. At the same time, I really believed that if Lisa didn't love me now, she would love me later. I would win her.

This wasn't the best of circumstances for starting a marriage, but to my relief, Lisa said yes. But the sting of her first response stayed with me for years. For the first decade of our marriage, whenever we had a fight, I'd accuse her of not loving me enough. "Well, you didn't want to marry me anyway!" I'd say. "You only agreed because I pushed you into it!" This was a tremendous insecurity of mine, and though Lisa and I always loved each other, it took a long time before enough trust built up for me to feel confident in her love for me.

Lisa and I got married in Houston on June 12, 1975, just two months after getting engaged. We didn't have much money, so we cut corners wherever we could: The ceremony was in her family's backyard, the reception was at my mom's studio, and Lisa made both her wedding gown and the three-piece suit I wore. She had been doing some sewing with a famous costume company in New York to make extra money, so she was able to make beautiful wedding clothes for both of us.

In photos taken during the ceremony, both Lisa and I have deer-in-the-headlights expressions. I think neither one of us could quite believe what was happening, and we both felt some fear about taking this step. Lisa cried through the whole wedding, except for one moment—when she tried to put my ring on and couldn't quite get it, she smiled a sweet little smile. As she stood there with tears in her eyes, all I could think was, "She's crying because she doesn't want to marry me." But she was actually just overwhelmed with emotion.

In fact, she later told me she had a realization during the ceremony. Looking at me, she had seen my vulnerability, and she suddenly had the thought that marrying someone is just about the nicest thing anyone can do for you. It's making a decision to hold nothing back. I was making a public vow to commit myself to Lisa forever, and she was touched by how profound that was. Unfortunately, I mistook the look on her face for horror, and I don't think I'm smiling in a single photo from our wedding ceremony.

Marrying Lisa was the best decision I ever made, and thirty-four years later I can say that it turned out better than I ever could have hoped. But looking back, I'm struck by how very young we were, and how little we really knew about each other, or anything, for that matter. There was a real passion between us, but that's not what made it last. It's the commitment we made—and kept—to work on the relationship as much as we needed in order to keep it going. Everybody goes through rough times, and we certainly ended up having our share, but we've always found a way to come back together, which is easier said than done.

Just as Lisa did, I found myself wondering whether, by getting married so young, I'd missed my opportunity to have real adventures in life. Right after high school, a friend and I had been offered the chance to crew a sailboat going around the world. We hadn't done it, and it was one thing that I feared I'd regret later on. Part of me wondered how many other opportunities I might miss out on now that I was married. But the other part of me was so happy to have found the woman I could ride off with into the sunset that nothing else mattered.

For our honeymoon, Lisa and I borrowed a motorcycle and rode to Lake Travis, about 180 miles outside Houston. We were pretty much broke, so we just camped and brought along a little cookstove for meals. We stayed for a week, and although it was about as low-cost as you could get for a honeymoon, we both had the time of our lives. For all the anxiety we'd felt at the wedding, we were happy and excited to begin our marriage together out in nature, just the two of us.

This was the beginning of our life's journey together. But as we discovered when we returned to New York, it wouldn't be all sunshine and roses.

# Chapter 4

Back in New York, the Harkness Ballet was sputtering to an end. Despite the support of Mrs. Harkness and the sparkling new theater at Lincoln Center, the company folded—and with it, my dreams of becoming a Harkness company dancer ended, too. Lisa had already left Harkness to train at the Joffrey Ballet, so she was set. But I needed to find a new place to continue pursuing my dream.

I managed to win a spot in the Eliot Feld Ballet, one of the most respected companies in New York. Every dancer in Eliot Feld was a soloist, so the quality of the dancing was extremely high. I was excited to join the company and immediately began striving to move up within it. I wanted to become a principal dancer, to get the best roles I could. The level of artistry in my dance was rising, and I wanted to make it to the top of the ballet world.

But as a letter from Lisa home to her mother describes, my knee problems were continuing to threaten my dance career:

*Yesterday Buddy went to a doctor because his knee was giving him a lot of trouble again. A Dr. Hamilton, really good,*

*specializes with dancers and has written books on their inju-*
*ries. The first of many, many doctors that Buddy felt he could*
*trust.*

  *Nothing really new about the knee except the arthritis has*
*set in faster than was expected. The bones are grinding flatter*
*and flatter. He was given lots of exercises and we bought a*
*brace to prevent it from moving too much. . . . He said he had*
*the knee of a 45-year-old man, and in five years it will be that*
*of a 100-year-old man. Cause for serious thinking. He might*
*not be dancing much longer, a year is the limit.*

This news had been especially painful to hear, because it came
just as I was making real headway with Eliot Feld. Lisa's letter
went on:

*Kinda awful because right now he's at a crossroads and it's*
*just now that things are rushing out to greet him. Eliot is crazy*
*over him, the things he has said to him are more than anyone*
*could hope to hear. Cora [Cahan, Eliot Feld's company man-*
*ager] says he's not just good on stage, he's fantastic. And he is,*
*and it's just now beginning to be noticed.*

But she also noticed something else, something deeper.
One thing I've always loved about Lisa is her ability to see beyond the obvious things. She's very intuitive and uncovers
things most other people can't see. And at this point, she was
realizing things about me that I didn't even see myself.

*One thing about Buddy is that he can be equally fantastic if he*
*does something else. His charisma, or whatever, shines as great.*
*I think it will turn out well, he doesn't have to stop dancing*

*altogether, just not be in a situation that demands too much.*
*And there are so many things he wants to do, but never has the*
*time: writing, his songwriting, is an important part of him.*

*Everything's kind of a blur right now, but something just*
*hits me that Buddy will bloom when he has the freedom to give*
*himself to all the things he wants to do. His reasons for danc-*
*ing confuse him so much. He can enjoy it, but something*
*drains him and downs him. As he said, this would show if it*
*was dancing or not. I, personally, at this point think that*
*dancing is a big part of him, but not his whole life, and that*
*makes him feel guilty. Something bothers him.*

Lisa was right—dancing was, and had always been, a source
of conflicting feelings for me. It stemmed from trying to please
my mother, from trying to make myself not just a good dancer
but the perfect dancer, and from pushing myself beyond my
limits. Everything Lisa said in this letter was true, and although
I didn't realize it yet myself, it was what would eventually save
me when I had to stop dancing full-time—a time that was
closer than I thought.

Meanwhile, our life in New York was a complete whirlwind.
Between rehearsals, teaching, singing, and side jobs, we were
constantly in motion. I've always been this way, trying to pack
in as much as I could in a day, but looking back I don't know
where we ever found the hours to sleep. We were so busy running around trying to make ends meet, to survive, to accomplish, that we were in overdrive all the time.

In addition to the dancing, training, and part-time jobs, we
also spent the first couple of years auditioning for musical theater roles during the ballet's off-season. I performed in *Music*
*Man* at the Paper Mill Playhouse in New Jersey, and did the

role of Riff in *West Side Story* at the Northstage Dinner Theatre in Long Island. But although these roles were fun to play and brought some money in, they were considered a step down for serious dancers. For a ballet dancer, the only real dancing is ballet—everything else just pales. Even dancing in Broadway shows.

Still, in 1975 I was happy to be cast as one of four featured dancers in *Goodtime Charley*. The show starred Joel Grey and Ann Reinking, and it ran for 104 performances. It was my first time dancing on Broadway—and also my first time meeting the cute, curly-haired young woman who would later play a big role in my life: Jennifer Grey. Jennifer is Joel's daughter, and she was fifteen that summer, a bubbly, outgoing, sweet girl. Neither of us could have known that twelve years later, we'd star together in a movie that would change both of our lives.

In the midst of our whirlwind of activities, Lisa and I still had just one overriding goal: to become principal dancers in a ballet company and achieve the highest possible level of artistry in dance. I hoped that the Eliot Feld Ballet would be the place I could do it.

Eliot Feld is one of the premier American choreographers of the last fifty years. He has choreographed more than 140 ballets and won numerous awards, including a Guggenheim fellowship and an honorary doctorate from Juilliard. He also can be a hard-nosed bastard, quick to berate his dancers and stingy with praise. Eliot sometimes used ridicule as a motivator, but when he expressed pleasure at something you'd done, it was the greatest feeling in the world.

I wanted more than ever to move up in the company, and

because of my knee, I knew it was now or never. Finally, in early 1976, I got my big break.

The company was planning to tour South America in May, but during rehearsals, Eliot's principal male dancer George Montalbano had to pull out because of injuries. That hole had to be filled in all the ballets he was dancing—and Eliot chose me to fill it. Suddenly, I was going to be performing principal roles in the South America tour, but that wasn't all. In addition to that, Eliot had big plans for the New York performances upon our return to the States. He started choreography on a new work that would have three company dancers—including me—dancing with none other than the great Mikhail Baryshnikov, who was coming in to perform as a guest star. This was a huge opportunity for a young dancer, the big chance I'd been waiting for.

Eliot started rehearsing me hard-core to get me ready, and I pushed myself even more, to a degree I hadn't thought possible. My knee was giving me as much trouble as ever, but I was determined to overcome it. A couple of months before the tour was to launch, I had one more knee surgery in an attempt to stabilize the joint. Looking back now, I can't believe how hard I worked my knee just after that surgery, and how much pain I forced myself to ignore. I also had no choice but to keep draining the knee, as it was swelling up as much as ever after eight to ten hours of rehearsing a day.

But as the tour dates drew near, I found myself having second thoughts about what I was putting myself through. Lisa and I had just gotten married, and I wasn't thrilled to be leaving her for two months. I'd even be missing our first wedding anniversary, which upset both of us. And I was afraid of getting my knee drained in South America, worried that conditions there would be less sanitary than those in New York. I'd already had my leg threatened by one staph infection, and I feared the same thing might happen again.

But could I really bow out of this amazing opportunity? After all the work and sweat of the last three years, I was going to tour South America with one of the most respected ballet companies in the world, not to mention performing back in New York with Baryshnikov. How could I possibly step away now? Wasn't this exactly what I'd been working for my whole life?

I decided to "cowboy up," ignoring all the pain and burying my worries. But then, one afternoon, a single freak incident changed everything.

I was riding my motorcycle on the West Side of Manhattan, heading downtown for a rehearsal on a bright, sunny day. The lanes narrowed as I approached the West Side Highway overpass, and suddenly a car cut right in front of me. I braked, but he'd cut too close—I had to maneuver to the left, trying to squeeze between his car and the guardrail. It was a dangerous moment, but it looked as if I'd managed to avoid a collision— until I suddenly saw a boy on a bicycle directly in my path. He'd been riding the wrong way down the street, and now there was nowhere for either of us to go as I careened toward him.

I knew in a flash we couldn't avoid colliding, so I instinctively hit the rear brake and let my motorcycle shoot out from under me, sliding sideways along the road. That way, the motorcycle would at least hit the kid's bicycle, rather than the kid himself. If we hit head-on, there was no doubt he'd be killed.

The maneuver worked perfectly: My motorcycle slammed into the boy's bike and he flew off, ending up with scratches but no serious injuries. I was okay, too—at least physically. I had some cuts and bruises, but was still able to rehearse that day. Emotionally, though, this accident really shook me up.

All the rest of that day, I was haunted by the thought that in that brief moment, if the accident had happened slightly differently, my dance career would have been over. When you're a professional dancer, everything hinges on your physical condition. I had worked my butt off, fighting pain and ignoring the signs of my body's rebellion—but none of that would have mattered if I'd hurt myself in that accident. It was as if I realized for the first time that my whole professional life hung by a thread, and that I'd been fooling myself thinking I could have a dance career with the knee problems I had.

The next day, I still couldn't shake these feelings, and all of a sudden I realized it was over. During a break in rehearsals, I talked to Cora Cahan. I broke down in tears, saying, "Cora, I don't think I can do this anymore," but she didn't want to hear it. She tried to talk me out of leaving, but I knew I was done. I just couldn't go on—not even for the chance to dance an important New York season with Baryshnikov. That week, I told Eliot I wouldn't be going on the South America tour, and just like that, my career as a professional ballet dancer was over.

It's hard to describe how devastating this decision was for me. I had worked so hard, and come so far, and just when it was all about to pay off I had to walk away. Even now, I get emotional thinking about it. With all the amazing experiences I've had as an actor, nothing really compares to the sense of joy and exhilaration dancing gives you. Leaving the ballet world created a void in me that I spent years trying to fill.

At the same time, I felt as if I'd let everyone down—Eliot Feld, the other dancers, my mother, Lisa, myself. I had wanted to be the best, and in the end it felt as if I had given up on my dream. Lisa tried to console me, pointing out that I'd gone incredibly far considering the injury and pain I was constantly dealing with. But it all sounded hollow, like lame justification. For so long I had been Patrick Swayze, aspiring ballet dancer. What would I do now?

Back when I was at San Jacinto Junior College, I'd had to deal with watching my dream of competing in the Olympics go down the tubes. That had been a huge disappointment, but it was not even close to the devastation I felt now. But fortunately, I had learned an incredible lesson from that first loss: When one dream dies, you have to move on to a new one. I could have fallen into serious depression when I left Eliot Feld, and very nearly did. But the lesson in self-preservation that I learned from that first disappointment saved me in the second one.

As I struggled to come to terms with my decision to leave the ballet world, two things kept me going. One was that I knew I had Lisa standing by my side, no matter what. The other was my growing interest in different spiritual philosophies, including Buddhist philosophy, which I had begun studying after I moved to New York.

Ever since I was a boy, I was always interested in the whole range of beliefs out there in the world. I'd gone to Catholic Masses growing up, and even considered becoming a priest at one point, but eventually I became disillusioned with Catholicism. The Catholic schools I'd attended were populated by the kind of mean nuns and knuckle-rapping priests you read about in books, which didn't do much to lead me further into the faith, and I even got in trouble once as an altar boy for sneaking sips of wine in the vestibule.

I always was curious about spirituality, though, so I started

exploring other options. In high school I devoured Kahlil
Gibran's writings, Antoine de Saint-Exupéry's *The Little Prince*,
and Eugen Herrigel's *Zen in the Art of Archery*. These books
spoke to me in a way church sermons didn't, and I drank them
in like a thirsty man. And because I had studied martial arts
for so long, I was also familiar with the notion of *chi*—the
search to connect with your true self.

Once I left Texas, I continued on this spiritual journey,
studying different belief systems and trying out new philosophies. New York in the 1970s was a hothouse of spiritual
exploration—everyone was looking for something to bring
meaning to their lives. Lisa and I spent a couple of weekends
doing est—Erhard Seminars Training—which was a hugely
popular, and controversial, seminar. Founded by Werner Erhard, the est system aimed to tear you down hard and then
build you back up to be better than you were, by teaching you
how to take responsibility for your own life and actions. The
training was wrenching, not least, as Lisa and I later joked,
because they wouldn't even let you go to the bathroom when
you needed to.

We did learn a lot from est, though—just as we learned a lot
from so many different philosophies we studied. One in particular that really spoke to me was Buddhism. I had begun
doing meditation and chanting, and found that not only did it
help me stay focused, it calmed the voices that were forever
trying to undercut me. What struck me about Buddhism was
that it didn't exclude other religions. You could be Catholic,
Jewish, or Hare Krishna and be Buddhist. And unlike some
religions, which require you to look outside yourself for God,
Buddhism was all about finding God from within—you have
everything you need within yourself. This philosophy had very

deep appeal for me, since I don't like having to depend on anyone for anything.

But the spiritual journey we were on wasn't about finding answers. It was about understanding the questions. Once you think you have the answers, you stop growing. Yet if you keep exploring, seeking, and opening your mind, you'll find that the learning never stops. This has helped me immeasurably in the difficult days of my life, from dealing with injury, to career disappointments, to the most trying days of all, as I fight to keep on living through cancer.

With my ballet career over, it was time to figure out the next dream. Performing was in my blood, and I wanted to continue doing it, so I began studying with Warren Robertson, one of the best acting coaches in New York. Lisa was still dancing, but she was broadening her horizons and had started doing TV commercials and auditioning for theater. She started studying with Warren, too, in anticipation of career opportunities to come.

Warren was an amazing teacher, perfect for young people because he knew how to break down your "act." Each of us has a way we present ourselves to the world—the "act" we show to other people as opposed to the true self, which we try to protect. Warren taught us that the degree to which you believe your own act is the degree to which you're limited in drawing from the deep well of characters inside you. This was especially liberating for me, because although I'd been acting since boyhood, it was almost always in musical theater—the "presentational" school of acting. Warren showed us a totally different approach, a more organic way of approaching acting.

Even as we studied with Warren, we kept one foot in the dance world by taking teaching jobs. Living on a shoestring in New York, Lisa and I would take whatever we could get—we taught jazz, acrobatics, and gymnastics classes in places as far-flung as Allentown, Pennsylvania; Fords, New Jersey; and Mt. Vernon, New York. We'd ride out on our motorcycle, whether through snow, rain, sleet, or whatever. The days were long and tiring, but the teaching brought in extra cash and kept us dancing.

Another way we made money was by doing woodworking and carpentry. Growing up, I had always enjoyed building things—the homemade motorbike was just one example—and while I was still at Harkness, I'd decided it would be a great idea to do a little carpentry on the side. I didn't know much about it, but that didn't stop me. How hard could it be, after all?

I had put word out that I was available for woodworking jobs, and it wasn't long before Bill Ritman, the set designer for Harkness, approached me with a potential job. Could I finish converting three floors of an Upper West Side brownstone into an apartment for him? I had to stop my mouth from falling open. This was a far bigger job than I'd anticipated—and it was for the Harkness set designer, who knew a little something about quality work. Any sensible person would have owned up to not having the experience, and perhaps not being up for it.

"Sure!" I told Bill. "Ready when you are!"

I'd showed up at the brownstone with a backpack full of tools, but unbeknownst to Bill, the most important tool of all was my *Reader's Digest* do-it-yourself carpentry guide. Let's just say I spent a lot of time in the bathroom on that first job, flipping through that book and trying to quickly teach myself how to do all the things Bill was asking me to do. Fortunately, it was a good guide, and I was a quick study. The brownstone work went off without a hitch, and I was on my way to making money as a carpenter and woodworker.

Lisa joined me in the woodworking business when I got a job building an entertainment center. I started working on it in our bedroom, and at some point I said to her, "Lisa, can you hold this board for me, please?" From that moment on, we were partners. We built that entertainment center together, and in the months to come we worked on tons of projects, doing the work in our bedroom (and ending up with sawdust in all our clothes) and stacking the finished projects in the living room. Our apartment ended up looking like a furniture showroom.

When we finished a project, we'd deliver it the same way we got everywhere else—on the motorcycle. We'd carry it down the five flights of stairs, and I'd get on the back of the motorcycle and try to balance whatever we'd made on my head while Lisa drove. I can remember carrying an artist's easel, about eight feet tall and four feet wide, on my helmet and just hoping it wouldn't tumble off into the traffic. Fortunately, we had a big motorcycle—a Honda four-cylinder K model, practically a car on a frame—so at least we weren't teetering along on a little bike.

Lisa and I got a decent number of woodworking jobs, thanks to recommendations from friends and the dance companies. But we still weren't making very much money, so every week we'd budget how much was coming in and how much we could spend. If we managed to have at least twenty dollars for food, that was a good week. And we always made sure we had a few dimes saved, in case we needed to make calls. The only way we had been able to get the motorcycle, in fact, was by managing to get a MasterCard and then immediately maxing out our credit limit to buy it. We spent the next five years paying off that debt.

We got very good at saving money, doing our shopping at the meat market downtown and making dishes that would keep. Lisa became an expert at making turkey last for days—she'd make turkey casserole, turkey tetrazzini, turkey sandwiches, turkey soup. When we got sick of turkey, she'd make hamburgers, pizza—whatever she could with the meager cash we had.

Every once in a while, we'd land a cool job that paid well, especially compared to the pennies we'd made as ballet dancers. Lisa and I got hired to sing and dance in industrial shows—trade shows for companies like Ford and Milliken Carpets, where we'd get flown to other cities, put up in hotels, and paid what felt like a fortune. Sometimes the companies even gave us samples of their products. Milliken, for example, gave us high-end area rugs—so although our apartment was sparsely decorated, a little dingy, and often covered with sawdust, we at least had beautiful rugs.

Around this time, I got in touch with a talent manager named Bob LeMond. Bob was originally from Houston, and my mother had helped get him into the managing business. I'd known Bob my whole life, and had always thought of him as just a quirky little guy from Texas, a would-be dancer who didn't dance nearly as well as he talked. But by 1977 he had become a big-time manager—he represented John Travolta, Jeff Conaway, Tony Danza, Barry Bostwick, and Marilu Henner, among others.

Bob's office was in Los Angeles, so I didn't call him the first couple of years I was in New York. But after rising in the dance world, and getting those musical theater credits under my belt, I decided it was time. I made an appointment through his secretary, and when we met in New York he had one question for me.

"Buddy, why didn't you call me before this?" he asked. "Where have you been?"

"Well, Bob," I said, "I wanted to wait until I felt I'd earned it. You know, I've always been Patsy Swayze's son, especially to you. I wanted to make a name for myself before coming in."

"That's your first mistake," Bob said. "You've got to use any-body you can in this business to get you where you want to go." I just looked at him, but he wasn't done yet. "Don't you ever do anything like that again in your career," he said.

Bob didn't take me on as a client just yet, but he told me he'd help me out. Right away I knew I was in good hands. He knew absolutely everybody in the business, and his charming, rather fey manner brought people's guard down. As one direc-tor I know joked years later, "You know, Bob and I would just talk, and he's got that southern thing and is so friendly, and we'd have such a good time—and then he leaves and I realize I just got screwed."

During the seventies, there was one show in particular that Bob used as a kind of breeding ground for his clients: the Broadway production of *Grease*. *Grease* had opened at the Broadhurst Theatre in 1972, and by the time I hooked up with Bob, it was on its way to becoming the longest-running Broad-way show in history. I hoped I might become Bob's latest pro-tégé to win a role in the show—and sure enough, before too long Bob had arranged an audition.

As Lisa revealed in a letter to her parents, we were both incredibly excited:

> *Buddy is up for (I don't know whether to say it or not) a role in Broadway's "Grease." It doesn't reveal itself on paper, but over here we're jumping up and down and screaming! He went to the audition and he's asked to come in and work on lines with the stage manager. As far as we know, there are two other guys up for the job. . . .*
>
> *Physically Buddy is the best choice, his voice and appearance couldn't be closer to what the role requires. He walked on stage and they said, "Danny Zuko!" They just have to see if he's an actor now. I guess we all do. I've never seen him do anything before. He has done acting but it was quite a while ago.*
>
> *It's a very big part, the lead as a matter of fact. He's perfect for the part, I know he could do it 'cause he's always playing around here exactly as Danny Zuko does on stage. He just has to do it for them. It's so exciting, I keep trying to stay objective and not start thinking of what it would do for him if he gets the part. I feel like I'm auditioning. Cross your fingers and we'll let everyone know.*

In that same letter, Lisa described the show she was currently in—a revival of *Hellzapoppin'*, which had been the longest-running Broadway musical back in the thirties and early forties. The revival starred Jerry Lewis and Lynn Redgrave, and Lisa was a featured dancer—but the New York critics savaged Lewis, who was politically unpopular at the time, and the show unfortunately never made it to Broadway.

Seeing her name printed on the programs, Lisa began to

wonder if "Haapaniemi" wasn't too much of a mouthful as a stage name. As she wrote to her parents:

*I like my name, it's my name, but I'm wondering how seriously people will take Haapaniemi, or what will happen if they ever have to put it on a marquee. I don't like the idea of people calling me another name, kind of like I like people to know me by Haapaniemi instead of only Swayze, but then what's best? I thought of shortening the last name like Happi or Niemi. Lisa Niemi, sounds Italian doesn't it?*

This was the first appearance of "Lisa Niemi" on paper— and before long, it would begin appearing on playbills and cast and crew lists, as Lisa embraced her new name and budding career as Lisa Niemi.

I won the role of Danny Zuko in late 1977, and started on January 3, 1978. The movie version starring John Travolta and Olivia Newton-John hadn't come out yet, but legions of theater patrons knew the story of Danny and Sandy from the show's nearly five-and-a-half-year run on Broadway.

In fact, during my time as Danny Zuko, *Grease* passed *Fiddler on the Roof* as the longest-running show on Broadway. Critics reviewed the show when we hit that milestone, and my performance got good reviews. I was doing eight shows a week— slicking my hair back with a combination of Groom 'n' Clean and hair spray, and singing, dancing, and acting my heart out. Although the schedule was exhausting, I loved being on Broadway—the excitement of the crowds, the adrenaline of performing live onstage. And for the first time, crowds started

gathering outside the stage door, waiting for me to sign autographs.

And there was another reason I was happy to be on Broadway: The paycheck was definitely bigger than what I'd been
making. Lisa and I had been saving our pennies for so long, it
was nice to finally have the cushion of a little more money. As
soon as we found out I'd gotten the role, we moved to a beautiful two-and-a-half-bedroom apartment up on 115th Street,
across from Columbia University. We still didn't have any furniture to speak of, but we did buy an actual bed—the first one
we ever owned together. No more sleeping on a mattress on
the floor!

Lisa and I loved our new place, and we loved New York. But
*Grease* began opening new doors for me, and soon enough
Bob LeMond planted the seed of an idea. He told us we should
come to Los Angeles, where he was based, to explore movies
and television. At first, neither of us was interested. As I told
an interviewer at the time, "I may love doing TV and movies,
but I don't want to leave New York—that's where the training
and creativity are." But as my eight-month stint in *Grease* began
winding down, we found ourselves thinking more seriously
about a move to Hollywood.

Lisa's theater career was just starting to take off, so this
would be an especially hard move for her. But she knew as well
as I did that we had to grab the momentum I'd gotten from
*Grease.* There were far more jobs for actors in Los Angeles than
in New York, so if we wanted to have a chance to seize that life,
now was the time. We discussed it and made the decision together that all things considered, this was the best move.

Over the course of a few months, we saved up about two
thousand dollars for the move. We called Bob to let him know

we'd be flying out to Los Angeles in a week or two. "Great!" he said. "Call me when you get here!" We booked our tickets, packed up our two cats and a couple of suitcases, and said good-bye to New York. Because we weren't sure things in California would work out, we sublet our apartment in case we needed to come back.

And with that, we were off to find our dramatic fortunes in Hollywood. Unfortunately, our first few days there would end up looking more like a comedy of errors.

# Chapter 5

After Lisa and I landed at LAX, the first thing we did was call Bob LeMond's office to tell him we'd arrived. Ivy Travis, an older English woman who worked at the agency, picked up the phone. She asked who was calling, and I told her "Patrick Swayze," expecting she'd recognize my name.

"I'm sorry," she said. "Who did you say you were?"

"Patrick Swayze," I said. "Bob just took me on as a client. My wife, Lisa, and I just flew in from New York."

"I see," she said. There was a pause. "Mr. LeMond is out of town and won't be back until next week."

This wasn't good news—we'd thought Bob would be able to help us find a place to stay and get settled in, but now he wasn't even going to be around. And in those pre-cellphone days, it wasn't that easy to get hold of people. We had no clue where to go—neither Lisa nor I had ever been to Los Angeles before.

"Well," I said, "would you happen to have any suggestions for a place we might stay? We don't really know the city."

"I believe most of our clients who come into town stay at the Beverly Hills Hotel," Ivy said. "I will let Mr. LeMond know you called." And with that, she hung up. Welcome to LA!

We made our way to the rental car counter, packed the cat carriers and suitcases in the car, and headed toward Beverly Hills. But as we drove along Sunset Boulevard by the Beverly Hills Hotel, we didn't even bother pulling in—it was a gorgeous hotel, obviously way beyond our means. We had a total of two thousand dollars, which had to last until we got work. Staying in that hotel, our money would have been gone within a week.

Lisa and I looked at each other, and though we didn't say it, we both were thinking the same thing. Had we made a mistake? We'd sublet our beautiful apartment in New York and left a wonderful life there, thinking Bob would take care of us. But he wasn't here, and his office didn't even know who I was. Had I misunderstood what he'd said?

We'd have to figure that out later, as right now we needed to find a place to stay. "Well, where should we go?" I asked Lisa.

"How about Hollywood?" she said. "That's why we're here, right?" So I took a quick look at the little map provided by the rental car company, and we made a U-turn to roll back down Sunset toward Hollywood.

Most people think of Hollywood as a glamorous place. And it is—but there are parts that are as seedy and run-down as any poor urban area. We pulled up to the first hotel we saw, and I went in to check on rates while Lisa waited in the car with the cats. I walked back to the car shaking my head.

"What's wrong?" Lisa asked.

"Well," I said, "they don't rent by the day."

She looked confused. "What does that mean?" she asked.

"Lisa, they only rent rooms by the hour," I said. Her eyebrows shot up as she understood what I meant, and I got back into the car and we took off.

Unfortunately, we ran into the same situation at the next two hotels we stopped at. Apparently, the only people looking to rent hotel rooms in Hollywood were using them for, shall we say, business purposes. By now, we were getting desperate. Darkness was starting to fall, and the streets of Hollywood seemed to be populated with hookers and junkies. Our cats were meowing in the backseat, and we were tired from our cross-country flight and the frustration of having nowhere to go. We felt like hamsters on a treadmill, with no clue how to get off.

Driving farther along Sunset Boulevard, we saw the Saharan Motor Hotel on the south side of the street and pulled in. I walked into the office, asked the man behind the front desk if he had any vacancies, and told him how desperate we were. "We just need a place for a few nights," I said. "Please, anything you've got."

"Well," he said, "I do have one lady who comes to town sometimes on business, and when she's not here, her room is available. But I'll have to call and ask if she's allergic to cats." I was ready to stand there while he dialed the phone, but he said, "Come back in an hour or so, and I'll have an answer for you." Reluctantly, we got back into the car and drove around some more. But when we came back, the man said the room was ours. Lisa and I had found our first "home" in LA.

At that time, the Saharan was the kind of place where you didn't want to walk barefoot on the carpet. It also was never quiet, even at night; you could hear the Laundromat next door, the sounds of prostitutes doing business in their rooms, and the occasional scream from the alleyway outside. Almost every night you'd hear somebody arguing, and sirens going by. But although the Saharan was pretty dire, the guy at the front desk was always smiling and kind. When we finally checked out a week or so later, after we'd found a place to rent, he said, "Come back and see us after you make it in Hollywood! You're welcome any time."

We managed to find a really nice apartment for cheap in the Hollywood Hills, in the lower half of a house owned by two women. It had a kind of bohemian glamour, and because it was built on a hillside, we had a fabulous view of Hollywood. The women upstairs were real characters, and one of them seemed always to have a tumbler of Scotch in her hand. Lisa and I both loved the apartment—but now we just had to find some work to pay the five-hundred-dollar-a-month rent.

Our two thousand dollars was going fast. Between staying those nights at the Saharan, paying first and last month's rent at our new place, and eating, we were just about broke. At night, I'd drive up to a spot on Mulholland Drive that had a beautiful panoramic view of Los Angeles. I'd sit there, looking out over the lights of Hollywood, and say, "I am going to conquer you." It was like a ritual every night, a way to gear myself up for the fight ahead. If I was going to make it in Hollywood, I had to really believe I could do it.

Thirty years later, I feel the same way about beating cancer. If I'm going to do it, I have to believe I can do it. So every single day I say, "I am going to conquer you." And every day, I believe it.


When Bob finally got back into town, he apologized for the mix-up and assured us he was taking me on as a client. He knew absolutely everybody in Hollywood, and right away, he started arranging interviews for me. I'd go to four or six a day, one right after the other, then come home and hope the phone would ring. Having performed in a lead role on Broadway certainly helped open doors, but it didn't guarantee that I'd get anything. But just at the moment our two thousand dollars had been whittled down to almost nothing, I got offered a role in a movie called *Skatetown, U.S.A.*

In the late 1970s, especially in Southern California, roller disco was king. You'd see skaters everywhere, half of them toting giant boom boxes playing the latest Earth Wind & Fire or Jackson 5 songs. Walking in Venice Beach, you'd be swarmed by skaters in bright socks and short-shorts, twirling their way down the boardwalk. So when I read the script for *Skatetown, U.S.A.*, I knew that even if it wasn't great art, it was at least part of a cultural phenomenon.

It also had a cast that included some of the hottest stars of the seventies: Scott Baio (Chachi from *Happy Days*), Maureen McCormick (Marcia from *The Brady Bunch*), Ron Palillo (Horshack from *Welcome Back, Kotter*), Melissa Sue Anderson (Mary Ingalls from *Little House on the Prairie*), and even the great comedians Flip Wilson and Ruth Buzzi. I was cast as Ace Johnson, the hot-shot, bad-boy skater in tight leather pants who battles the hero, Stan, played by Greg Bradford.

I had roller-skated competitively in my teens, but hadn't done much since then. I was hell-bent on doing some amazing things on skates for this movie, so I had my dad send me my top-of-the-line figure skates from Houston and began practicing moves on any open paved area I could find. I spent hours honing moves, from camels to double Salchows. By the time we started filming, I was pumped—I wanted to bust Hollywood wide open with my first role.

Unfortunately, I almost busted my ass on my first stunt. I

was supposed to jump over a Fiat parked at the end of the Santa Monica pier, using a small ramp. I raced down the pier, going faster and faster, and when I hit that ramp I shot up into the air—a lot higher than I expected to. In the footage, you can see me yell "Charge!" as I take off, then the look on my face changes from determination to wide-eyed surprise. The camera cuts away before showing me landing, flat on my back, on the cement. I had the breath knocked out of me, but we did get it in one take.

My scenes at the roller rink with April Allen, where I could show off my dance training as well as skating, went more smoothly. April was a world-champion roller skater whom I'd skated with years earlier in Houston. We were friends from way back, so I couldn't believe it when it turned out we'd be performing together in my first movie.

April was an amazing skater, and she and I heated up the set with a skate-dance scene that was powerful, sensual, and sexy. I also had a solo skate that led to the review that launched my career, when Kevin Thomas of the *Los Angeles Times* wrote, "Not since John Travolta took the disco floor in *Saturday Night Fever*—no, not since Valentino did his tango in *The Four Horsemen of the Apocalypse*—has there been such a confident display of male sexuality as when a lithe newcomer to films named Patrick Swayze hits the rink . . . Swayze drew gasps [and] ought to be on [his] way in films."

This was flattering, of course, but on another level it was the last thing I wanted. I wanted to be a serious actor, not a dancer-turned-actor or hunk-of-the-week. Not long after *Skatetown* came out, Columbia offered me a multipicture deal to star in teen idol–type movies, but after talking about it with Lisa, I turned it down. We both knew that if I accepted, even though the money would be fantastic and it would be guaranteed work, no one would ever take me seriously as an actor.

As I had just arrived in Hollywood, it was definitely hard to turn down a multipicture deal. But Bob LeMond gave me a piece of advice that made it easier. "The only power you have in this business," he told me, "is the power to say 'no.' More careers have been screwed up by 'yes' than anything else." I took Bob's advice to heart and said no to Columbia, and turned my attention to finding better roles.

But to my frustration, the one role I really wanted that year was one I couldn't have: Bud Davis in *Urban Cowboy,* which was filming in Houston at the same time I was shooting *Skatetown, U.S.A.*

Bud Davis was a Texas cowboy who loved to dance—a role that had my name all over it. But John Travolta was flying high with his successes in *Saturday Night Fever* and *Grease,* and the part was his for the taking. It tore me up to think of what I could have done with that character, and how it would have launched my career. It was also frustrating because my mother was the choreographer for *Urban Cowboy,* and she had hired Lisa to work with her. So Lisa was working down in Houston on the movie I'd wanted, while I was in LA alone finishing up *Skatetown, U.S.A.*

As soon as we wrapped, I flew down to Houston to join Lisa. One night we ended up hanging out with John and teaching him a few steps, which frustrated me even more. Country dancing was in my DNA, and as much as I liked John, I hated giving someone else tips on how to play a role I was born for. But really, what I hated was that he was so good at it. John was an absolute natural—he was like a sponge who just picked everything up. He's also a generous and kind-hearted person, and both Lisa and I liked him right away. We became good friends on that movie and have been friends ever since.

After I turned down the Columbia deal, I kept auditioning for other, better roles. I got my first TV role in the made-for-TV movie *The Comeback Kid,* starring John Ritter and Susan Dey. It aired in the spring of 1980, and though I was proud of my work, I still wanted more—bigger, better roles. I got my wish after *The Comeback Kid,* when I won a part on *M\*A\*S\*H*.

*M\*A\*S\*H* was a long-running, incredibly popular show— but that wasn't what got me so excited about working on it. It was the fact that *M\*A\*S\*H* was very well respected in the industry, with talented actors like Alan Alda, Loretta Swit, Harry Morgan, and Mike Farrell. Winning a part on *M\*A\*S\*H* meant that the producers believed you could hold your own among the cast. Playing Private Gary Sturgis was my first great role in Hollywood, and oddly enough, it had a plot twist involving cancer.

Most of my scenes took place with Alan Alda, who played Dr. Hawkeye Pierce. My character, Private Sturgis, has hurt his arm in combat. He gets sent to the *M\*A\*S\*H* unit at the same time as his buddy, who's more severely injured and needs a blood transfusion. Sturgis desperately wants to give blood to his buddy, knowing they share the same blood type. But Hawkeye tests Sturgis's blood and discovers he has leukemia. When Hawkeye tells him, Sturgis breaks down—he had no idea he was ill.

Playing Sturgis was an amazing experience for me. Everyone on the set was incredibly professional, and it was a dream to act opposite Alan Alda in my scenes. I just followed his lead, and the emotion poured out of me. Using the process I'd learned in my acting classes, I was able to tap deep wells of anger and bitterness at how unfair the diagnosis was for this young kid. It was an emotional experience, and I felt very proud of the work when I saw the finished episode.

But through those first two years in LA, parts like that were few and far between. I kept holding out for good roles, but as a result, I wasn't working as much as I wanted to. In the meantime, Lisa and I acted together in a play, *The Brick and the Rose,* at the Attic Theatre on Santa Monica Boulevard. We both got good reviews, with the *LA Weekly* writing that "Dennis Visca and Lisa Niemi stand out in a superb supporting cast that slides in and out of 45 roles . . . and Patrick Swayze, a gifted L.A. newcomer, brings more to the starring role than I would have thought possible. Bravo!"

Doing plays doesn't pay the bills, though, so Lisa and I started up our woodworking business again on the side. We built stage sets for *I'm Dancing as Fast as I Can,* starring Jill Clayburgh, Dianne Wiest, and Geraldine Page. We also did some work for Jaclyn Smith, whom I knew well from Houston. Jackie had been a student at my mom's studio in the seventies, but now she was a Hollywood star thanks to her starring role on *Charlie's Angels.* Yet she never acted like a big star—she was always welcoming and warm to Lisa and me, and supported us however she could, even making an appearance at the premiere of *Skatetown, U.S.A.*

Meanwhile, my parents had left Houston, too. After working on *Urban Cowboy,* my mom decided she wanted to choreograph more Hollywood movies, so she and my dad pulled up their Texas roots and moved to Simi Valley, just north of Los Angeles. I was happy to have my parents nearby, even though our busy schedules kept us from seeing each other all that often.

But even having my parents just up the road didn't help when, during our second year in LA, Lisa and I suddenly found ourselves in an unexpected situation: dead broke, without even enough money to eat.

Lisa and I had been working pretty steadily on carpentry jobs, but the pay was minimal compared to the hours we put in. The rest of our time was taken up with auditions, acting classes, and other nonincome activities. Somehow, we must have lost track of our income and expenses, because one day around Christmas, Lisa checked our account and discovered we had about three dollars left. We were still expecting a little bit of money for a job we'd just finished—but that was already earmarked for rent and bills.

All of a sudden, we realized there was no money to go home to Texas to visit Lisa's family for Christmas, no money for presents, no money even for food to eat.

"How the hell did this happen?" Lisa asked. She did a quick update of our bank statements and checkbook—something we should have done months before. Our monthly expenses stood at about twelve hundred dollars, which was a huge sum compared to what we'd been spending in New York.

After a year or so of living in the Hollywood Hills, we had moved into an apartment in West Hollywood, on La Jolla Avenue. The saving grace of our new apartment was the orange tree in the backyard, which ended up feeding us for the difficult weeks we spent trying to pull our financial life together. We managed to scrape together enough coins to buy a jar of peanut butter and a loaf of bread, and that, with the oranges, was what we ate.

Although my parents were in Simi Valley, I was too proud to ask them for money or food—I didn't even want them to know we were in such dire straits. Lisa did tell her mom what was going on, but her family was strapped at the time, too, and couldn't send anything to tide us over. The couple of times when friends invited us over for dinner, we didn't let on how hungry we were—we just tried to act as if everything was normal. But we were completely demoralized, and once again found ourselves wondering, had we made a big mistake leaving New York? We had never been this desperate there.

There's a difference between simply being broke, and being broke while not knowing where your next paycheck will come from. After working our butts off for two years in Hollywood, we didn't have any new work on the horizon. We started looking around at what we could sell to get enough money for food, which just about killed whatever sliver of optimism we might have had left. There's a kind of despair that sets in when you feel that you've failed in reaching your biggest goal. And that's what Lisa and I felt like. I thought of those nights I'd sat out on Mulholland Drive, vowing to conquer Hollywood, and bitterness rose in my throat.

We had done some carpentry work for an older man named Mr. Green, so in a last-ditch effort to make some quick money, we called him and threw ourselves on his mercy. "Do you have anything that needs doing?" I asked him. "Anything at all?" And Mr. Green, sensing the desperation in my voice, came up with a laundry list of small tasks for us. The biggest was building a doghouse for his two German shepherds, a task Lisa and I jumped on as soon as I hung up the phone.

But just as in a Hollywood movie, real life in Hollywood can change in an instant. In the midst of our despair, as we toiled away on the doghouse for the few dollars that would tide us over, I got a call about a new TV show I'd auditioned for a few weeks earlier. It was called *The Renegades*—and I was being offered a leading role!

Just like that, I soared from the depths of despair to the heights of euphoria. Getting a role on a TV series was a huge leap for a struggling young actor, bringing with it the promise of job stability and a really good paycheck for the foreseeable future. I couldn't believe my luck. And I couldn't wait to tell Lisa.

But first, I made a stop at a place I'd wanted to go for the past two years—an auto dealership selling DeLoreans. These were the gull-winged cars designed by John DeLorean, who made only nine thousand of them before shutting down production in 1982. In the early 1980s, the DeLorean was the emblem of style and slick automotive design, and I'd wanted one ever since the prototype came out in the mid-1970s. With my new job, and if I could manage to talk them down in price, the car would finally be within my means. So I went straight to the dealership, and then called Lisa.

"Hey, Lisa," I said. "I've got some news for you."

"What?" she said, probably expecting anything but what I said next.

"I'm buying a DeLorean."

"You're *what*?!" she said, surprise and excitement in her voice. She knew there had to be more—either that, or I'd completely lost my mind.

"I got a part on *The Renegades!*" I said, and whooped. It was such a great moment—the kind that Hollywood dreams are made of. And it was all the more amazing because it came just when we'd been on the edge of despair. Lisa was thrilled, though she did have one concern.

"Shit," she said. "Now I'm going to have to build that dog-house all by myself!"

After I bought the car, Lisa and I drove up to Simi Valley to show it off to my parents. I'll never forget my dad's response when he came out to see us pulling up in the sparkling new DeLorean, with its signature stainless-steel panels and flat, square hood.

"Well, what are you doing driving around in a kitchen sink?" he asked, a big smile on his face. It was obvious how proud he was of me at that moment, and that was worth more than any role or any car would ever be. It was one of the best moments of my life.

# Chapter 6

*T*he *Renegades* was an updated version of *The Mod Squad,* a groundbreaking cop series that ran between 1968 and 1973. I played Bandit, the tough-talking leader of a gang of street thugs, although in my tight leather pants and sleeveless vests, I looked as much model as tough guy. Shooting *The Renegades* was definitely fun, and I was happy to have steady TV work. But I still wanted to find roles that would stretch me more as an actor.

All things considered, though, things were looking up. I was making good money, and Lisa and I were taking acting classes with the respected teacher Milton Katselas. We loved our apartment on La Jolla Avenue, and our circle of friends was growing steadily. Almost three years after moving to LA, we at last felt like we were settling in. We even made plans to finally move the rest of our stuff from New York.

Then, one day when I came home from shooting, everything came crashing down.

I pulled into our driveway and walked into the two-car garage we'd turned into our woodworking shop. I'd just started messing around with a project we were working on when I felt

Lisa walk up behind me. To this day I couldn't tell you how I knew it, but I knew right away something was very wrong. Lisa put her hand on my shoulder and said, "Buddy, could you come into the house? I need to tell you something."

I wheeled around. "What is it?" I said. "Tell me now." I could see she'd been crying, and I felt the blood drain from my face.

"Your mom called," she said quietly. "Your dad had a heart attack. He's dead."

My knees buckled, and I sank to the floor. As soon as the words were out of Lisa's mouth, I was sobbing, crying like I'd never cried before. I felt sick, like I'd been sucker-punched in the stomach. I don't know how long I was on the floor, but it felt like I might never be able to get up again.

"He was walking with the dogs out behind their house," Lisa said, rubbing my back. "He died instantly. There was no pain." This would be a small consolation later, but I wasn't ready to be grateful for anything yet. I just couldn't believe my dad was gone.

My dad, the gentle cowboy, was my source of unconditional love while I was growing up, the steady hand on the rudder. My mother loved us with a fierce, proud, demanding love, while my father loved us without question or qualification. Big Buddy had taught me what it meant to be a man, and he'd shown me that a real man could be tough and gentle at the same time. Seeing his example growing up was a huge influence on me, and I loved him all the more for it.

Born and raised in Wichita Falls, in the Texas Panhandle, my dad had grown up on a small working ranch. There, he learned how to do all the things a cowboy does—doctor and brand cattle, repair fences, ride and groom horses. He was a cowboy in his blood, not just for show. And although his life wasn't easy and they never had much money growing up, he always had a smile and a good word for everyone. In turn, everyone loved Buddy Swayze.

Dad and I had always loved being outdoors, and it was comforting in some ways that he died outside, with his dogs, in the beauty of nature. We used to go out into the wilderness together, with just a few supplies and his knowledge of living off the land to sustain us. I treasured those days with him, exploring the landscape and learning the most basic human ability: how to exist in the natural environment. I've always been proud of the skills I learned with him, and I still think of him whenever I'm outside, living off the land, or even just appreciating the sights and smells of nature.

As stabilizing a force as my father had been in life, his death had the opposite effect on me. Everything was suddenly off-kilter, and the pain I felt seemed bottomless. I'd never been much of a drinker, but one of the first things I did after my dad died was buy a case of his favorite beer, Budweiser. I hated the taste, but I popped open can after can, trying to get myself drunk. No matter how much I drank, I couldn't feel anything. So I kept drinking.

My dad's death was devastating for many reasons. For one thing, it just about killed my mother, who had loved and depended on him for all those years. She was crushed, and felt angry and alone without the man who'd always been there to support her. My mother is a strong woman, but her emotions run strong, too. And losing him nearly put her over the edge with grief. My brothers and sisters were devastated, too, especially Donny and Sean. Losing a parent is hard. But losing a father who was the embodiment of what you want to become as a man is crushing.

For me, my father's death meant my very identity had changed. My whole life, he'd been Big Buddy and I was Little Buddy. But now that he was gone, I'd have to be the Big Buddy—I was the oldest male in the family, and now I had to step up and be a man. This marked a new level of responsibility, and it started right away. Lisa and I had to plan my father's funeral and take care of all the details leading up to it. This was difficult enough, but there was one truly horrible moment that showed me just how strong I'd need to be.

It happened just before the viewing at the funeral home. I went down before the rest of the family arrived, to make sure the undertakers had prepared his body and everything was set. But when I looked in the casket, I was shocked. The man lying there looked nothing like my father—they had put too much blush makeup on his otherwise pale face, and his normally wavy hair was straight and stiff. He looked like a clown, I thought, as rage rose in my chest. And I knew it would kill my mother to see him this way.

"Take him back there," I said to the undertaker, my voice tight. "I'll do his makeup myself."

And in the back room of that funeral home, I gently wiped my dad's face while the tears streamed down my own. I desperately wanted to make him look like my dad again, but I just couldn't get it—until finally, after a few fits and starts, I got the makeup right and managed to fix his hair the way he always wore it. When I was finished, I wiped the tears from my eyes and took him back out for the viewing. It was the hardest thing I'd ever done.

We buried my father in a simple wood casket rather than a fancy hermetically sealed one, as it just seemed right to let nature take its course, from dust to dust. I don't remember much about the funeral, but I remember wanting to carve his initials into the casket just before we lowered it into the ground. I didn't end up doing it, and regretted it. He'd always carried an Old Timer knife, and I did, too—it was part of our identities as Swayze men. But when that last moment came, I just watched as the casket was lowered, and then we threw dirt over it, and he was gone.

In the months after my dad died, I began drinking like I'd never done before. I was trying to get drunk, but I never could feel it. In some strange way, I felt like I was honoring my dad, by doing something he loved to do—drinking beer. Like many men of his era in Texas, my father drank a lot, probably too much. And in some ways, I think I was trying to see how much like him I really was.

One thing about being a Swayze is, you never do anything halfway. Lisa was concerned about how much I was drinking, but I didn't want to stop. Late at night, I'd take my DeLorean up to Mulholland Drive—the twisting, steep part through the Hollywood Hills where car aficionados would come to race. I'd put a case of beer on the seat beside me and go, taking on any and all comers to do suicide runs up and down Mulholland. I never got into an accident, maybe because I never felt as impaired by the alcohol as I probably was. But all the same, it wasn't safe or smart, and Lisa was understandably worried about me.

In all my life, I never drank for the sake of drinking; it was always a response to some kind of emotional difficulty I was going through. Drinking for me was a symptom of a problem, not the problem itself. But it certainly caused problems between Lisa and me, as she grew increasingly worried about my behavior. She would plead with me to cut back, but I felt a deep, unstoppable need to go through with what I was doing. Every time a memory of my dad popped into my brain, it turned into a fresh, open wound again. His death had thrown me completely off balance, and I didn't know how to cope with it.

All the insecurities I'd felt over the years came crashing down on me. I was still trying to find an identity for myself. Who was I? Was I just some teen idol, a piece of beefcake who'd never be taken seriously as an actor? Then what was all my training for? When my father was alive, I had his unconditional love to anchor me. I don't think I even realized how much I'd counted on it. But now that it was gone, I felt the huge void left by its absence. And I felt angry, as if he'd abandoned me.

Lisa loved me unconditionally, too, but I wouldn't let myself believe that. I still felt stung by her initial response when I'd asked her to marry me. Our relationship has always been passionate, in both positive and negative ways—our love for each other was incredibly intense, but so were our fights. This was the first really tough period in our marriage, and the intensity of it scared us both.

I knew all too well what had happened to so many creative artists—James Dean, Janis Joplin, Freddy Prinze, Jim Morrison, Jimi Hendrix—who got swallowed by their ambitions and destroyed by the choices they made. I had studied their examples to make sure I didn't end up going down that road myself. But as I soon discovered, whatever you resist, persists. I was drinking too much to prove I didn't have to drink too much, in a cycle I didn't know how to stop.

So I did the only thing I knew to do: I buried myself in my

"Little Buddy" Swayze, age five.

My parents, Buddy and Patsy Swayze, with my older sister, Vicky, my little brother Donny, and me.

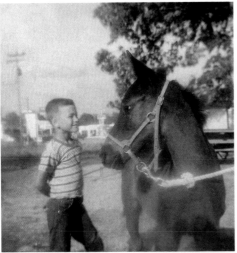

With my beloved Arabian Zubi. As the son of a cowboy, I loved horses from the time I could walk.

Showing off at my mom's dance studio at age sixteen.

I loved football and even thought I might play in
college. But one fateful game changed my life forever.

Little Lisa Haapaniemi, already
a dancer at age three.

The Nordic brood gathers: the Haapaniemi family. Edmond, Sr.; Paul; Alex;
Ed; Lisa; John; grandmother Aili; Eric; and mom, Karin.

Teenaged Lisa was the most beautiful girl I had ever seen. If only I could figure out how to talk to her.

Despite the fact that I pinched her butt when we first met, she eventually came around and started to like me, too. (Photo: *Houston Chronicle*. Copyright © *Houston Chronicle*)

In the Disney on Parade traveling show
in the early 1970s, I played Prince Charming.

Lisa moved to New York in the summer of 1974.
We shared the dream of becoming top-flight
ballet dancers.

Keeping my knee in dance shape was a constant challenge. Here, I'm lifting weights among the cabinets Lisa and I built in our small New York apartment.

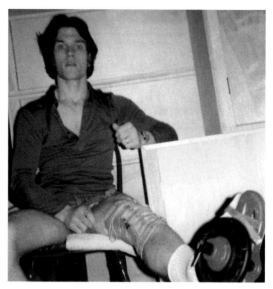

My Honda 750 was our main mode of transportation, even for cross-country trips.

At our wedding in June 1975. This was the only moment
during the ceremony that Lisa smiled—when she had trouble
getting the ring on my finger.

Short on money, we held the reception at
my mom's dance studio.

Toasting the bride. It took years before I was convinced she
really did love me as much as I loved her.

Lisa backstage, dressed for her part in
*Hellzapoppin'*, starring Jerry Lewis.

During our time in New York, I played guitar
and sang in the clubs of Greenwich Village.

Dancing with Lisa in New York. The training was exhausting
and physically demanding—but it was also exhilarating.

Our first "home" in Los Angeles: The Saharan Motor Hotel on Sunset Boulevard in Hollywood. (Photo by Lisa Dickey)

My first movie role, as Ace Johnson in 1979's *Skatetown USA*, featured a sexy skate-dance that turned critics' heads. ("SKATETOWN USA" © The Skatetown Company. All Rights Reserved. Courtesy of Columbia Pictures)

Lisa and me with our cats Scooter and Benois, in our apartment on La Jolla Avenue. I'm wearing a T-shirt from my first TV show, *The Renegades*.

My mom stands with Lisa and me outside our apartment on La Jolla. At this time, she and Lisa were working together on *Urban Cowboy*.

When I got the role on *Renegades*, a few weeks after
Lisa and I realized we were broke, I celebrated by
buying a DeLorean.

My dad, Jesse "Buddy" Swayze, was a strong
but gentle cowboy who was loved by all.

Little Buddy and Big Buddy. When my father died in 1982, I swore I'd spend the rest of my life trying to make him proud every day.

The Swayze family. Clockwise from top left: Me, Donny, Sean, Vicky, Bambi, Dad, and Mom.

My first important break came with Francis Ford Coppola's *The Outsiders*, which featured some of the hottest up-and-coming actors around, including Emilio Estevez, C. Thomas Howell, Rob Lowe, and Tom Cruise. ("THE OUTSIDERS" © Pony Boy, Inc. Licensed by: Warner Bros. Entertainment Inc. All Rights Reserved)

work. At my dad's funeral, I'd made a vow to live in a way that would have made him proud. The moment when he beamed at me in my new DeLorean was forever burned into my memory, and I wanted to continue to live as if he was watching me. From that time on, that's what I've tried to do.

After I became an actor, I realized my life had a certain pattern to it. In high school, I had worked to become the best football player I could be—and once I hit the top, winning a couple of football scholarships, I stopped playing. I then turned to gymnastics, and the same thing happened: I was working toward the Junior Olympics, at the top of my game— and then I stopped competing. At Eliot Feld, I was offered the chance to perform at the pinnacle of the ballet world, dancing onstage with the legendary Mikhail Baryshnikov. And once I'd made it there, I left.

In all these cases, my decision to leave came partly because of injury. But I also realized that, in reaching these pinnacles, I feared that whatever came next would be a letdown. After you make the Olympics, what's next? Your face on a Wheaties box? After you dance with Baryshnikov, what's next? I always needed a goal, something to push toward. And I feared what would happen to me if I reached the top of a given profession, and then had nowhere else to go.

But acting was different. For the first time, I was throwing myself into something that could never be mastered. Acting wasn't like sports—you didn't win the world championship and then settle into retirement. No matter how great an actor you are, you can *always* be better. Every role is different, and the learning curve is endless. I was excited to find something that would never stop challenging me and humbled by the chance to make a living at it.

And soon after my father died, I would have a chance to stretch my acting ability even further, by working with one of the greatest film directors in history, Francis Ford Coppola.

The auditions for *The Outsiders* were unlike any auditions I'd ever been to before. Based on the best-selling book by S. E. Hinton, *The Outsiders* focused on a group of "Greasers"—a gang of high school toughs trying to find their way in the world. Throughout the movie, the Greasers clash with the "Socs"—pronounced "soshes," short for the social upper-class kids. It's a classic coming-of-age story, fueled by testosterone and violence, and Francis wanted to find young male actors who could disappear into those characters.

The movie's climactic scene is a giant fight, or "rumble," between the two factions. So for the auditions, Francis invited dozens of young actors to stage improvised fights on a soundstage. Usually when you audition, you're alone in a room with the casting director, director, and maybe a few other people. Auditioning with a huge group of talented young actors brought out the competitive fire in everyone. And because Francis was a legend, having already made *The Godfather* and *The Godfather II* as well as *Apocalypse Now*, everybody was pumped to impress him.

There was method to his madness, because he ended up with an amazing cast of up-and-coming male actors. Matt Dillon, C. Thomas Howell, Rob Lowe, Emilio Estevez, and Ralph Macchio all played Greasers, as did a young Tom Cruise, in only his third movie role. Matt Dillon was already a budding star, having played lead roles in *Little Darlings*, *My Bodyguard*, and *Tex*, but the rest of us were just starting out. And we were anxious to make our mark.

We lived these roles, staying in character almost all the time. We became like a gang ourselves, hanging out together, smoking cigarettes, going out for drinks, and just generally running wild. Those were crazy days on Hollywood lots, with drugs, alcohol, and testosterone fueling everything—though the Greasers' drug of choice was beer. And Francis ratcheted things up a notch with his style of directing, which was aimed at bringing out the most realistic emotions possible.

Francis was all about instinct and the pursuit of perfection. He was one of the most demanding directors I've ever worked with, and he stopped at nothing to get the performance he wanted. He'd talk to you and draw you out, finding your deepest, darkest secrets. Then, on set, he'd announce them over a loudspeaker for everyone to hear. This had the effect he wanted—my blood would pound when I'd hear his voice over that speaker—but it's a brutal way to bring out an emotional performance.

Francis and I also clashed after I asked him about camera angles for a couple of scenes. I was curious about the art of filmmaking, and here I was working with the master—I figured it was as good a time as any to ask questions and learn how it was done. But when I asked him about why he chose to shoot in certain ways, he misunderstood why.

"Ah, everyone knows that all dancers are interested in is looking at themselves in the mirror," he said to me.

This was a real insult, and it was all the worse coming from a legendary director. I didn't care about how my face looked onscreen—I wanted to be the best actor I could. And if he didn't believe that was so, why had he cast me? Francis's comment really pissed me off, but there wasn't much I could do about it, except show him how hard I would work in my performance. Which is probably what he was angling for in the first place.

With all that said, I loved Francis and would have worked with him on anything. He brought out performances we never thought possible. Anything went on that set—it was as if he'd given us all permission to create these amazing characters and live in their skin. The climax of it all was the final "rumble" between the Greasers and Socs, where we didn't just act out a massive gang fight. We really *had* a gang fight, with fists flying and blood running and guys pounding on each other.

Francis brought in a bunch of local kids, and on a day when the rain came pouring down, he put us all together in a giant muddy lot to battle it out. He whipped us up, telling us to make it as realistic and violent as possible, and when he set us loose, everyone went crazy. Guys were beating on each other, punching and kicking and wrestling in the mud. In the middle of it, one guy came charging at me with a wild look in his eyes. He was coming to lay me out, and the only way I could keep from getting hurt myself was to hurt him. I punched him hard in the face and knocked him unconscious.

There was actually some choreography planned for the rumble, with each of us fighting specific people, but by the end everybody was just whaling on everybody else. But the really interesting thing was that all of us Greasers stuck together, watching each other's backs like this was a real gang fight. Our survival instincts kicked in, and we fought with a kind of primal animal fury. It was a brilliant, reckless piece of filmmaking, and by the end of it we felt as bonded as any real gang.

Tom Cruise had the smallest role of any of us, but he worked harder than anyone. Even then, at age twenty and with very few credits to his name, he was as driven as anyone I'd ever seen. For the scene in the movie where the Greasers are heading out to the rumble, Tom's character does a backflip off a car in excitement. I taught Tom that move, and in fact Lisa and I taught most of the other Greasers a few gymnastics moves to use in the rumble. I was the big brother in the movie, and I felt like one on the set, too.

I also taught Emilio, Tommy, Ralph, and Rob how to hop freight trains. Growing up, I used to hop freight trains to Galveston so I could go surfing at the beach there. There's an art to it: You have to pick a spot where the train will slow down, such as a freight yard or residential area, and then time your jump so you sail into the open door rather than under the train. We spent a lot of time together, shooting pool and just hanging out, most often in character.

I had a blast working with all the guys, and I particularly bonded with Tommy Howell. We'd met on the set of *Urban Cowboy*, where his dad was a stuntman, and we had a shared love of the cowboy life. Tommy was a true cowboy—he loved horses and had even been a junior rodeo champion, and he and I remained close after *The Outsiders*. In fact, over the next year and a half, we would act in two more films together: *Grandview, U.S.A.* and *Red Dawn*.

When *The Outsiders* came out, the posters and promotional materials showed all the Greasers posing in denim and leather, looking tough with our hair slicked back. We all got a lot of attention from the film, including the inevitable *Teen Beat* and *Tiger Beat* magazine photo spreads for girls. Tom Cruise didn't want to do those photo shoots, since he was self-conscious about his teeth and thought he wasn't good-looking enough. But he got roped into it just like the rest of us, and before long, he became the biggest movie star of all.


One thing I've always loved about being an actor is getting the chance to travel all over the world for work. In the course of our careers, Lisa and I have been fortunate enough to travel to places as far-flung as India, Namibia, Hong Kong, Russia, and South Africa, as well as beautiful locations all across the United States. It was just after *The Outsiders* that we got to travel to our first exotic location—Thailand—for the 1984 film *Uncommon Valor*. I traded in the first-class airplane ticket the studio bought me for two economy seats, so Lisa could join me in Bangkok.

Starring Gene Hackman and Robert Stack, *Uncommon Valor* was about a group of Vietnam veterans who return to Southeast Asia to rescue a buddy who'd been taken prisoner in the war. I was excited to be working with Gene Hackman, who was already a huge star thanks to his roles in movies as diverse as *The Conversation, The Poseidon Adventure, The French Connection, Bonnie and Clyde*—and the list went on. Getting this role was another step in the right direction, continuing the momentum that was starting to build in my career.

It was a big break to be cast with Gene, and he took me under his wing on the set. He was unfailingly professional and very generous with his time and insight. He also taught me a very big lesson about acting, telling me, "You're not here for yourself. You're only here to serve." This fed right into everything I'd studied in Buddhism—that it's only through learning to serve that you can become a master. Gene devoted himself to his movies—even if it took twenty takes for the other actor to get it right, Gene would be right there, delivering his lines with the same energy and dedication. Every single time. It was mesmerizing to watch him work.

Meanwhile, my role called for as much fighting as acting. I played a cocky young Special Forces soldier who's brought in to train the Vietnam vets. On the set, I was taught by ex–Special Forces guys, learning hand-to-hand combat techniques from the best in the world. In addition to traveling, that's another of the things I love best about my job—getting the chance to learn new skills from the top experts in each field. I've been lucky enough to study martial arts, kick-boxing, surfing, skydiving, and many other skills on movie sets. It's been like having my own personal training to become Doc Savage, my childhood hero.

For one scene in *Uncommon Valor*, I fought a character played by Randall "Tex" Cobb—a former boxer turned actor who'd gone fifteen rounds with heavyweight champion Larry Holmes just a year earlier. Tex's character in the movie, Sailor, was crazy—but no crazier than Tex himself. He was a classic barroom-brawler type, a huge man with a fleshy nose that lay flat against his face, supposedly because he'd had the cartilage removed so he could take more punches. The beating Tex had taken in his fight with Holmes had been so severe, Howard Cosell had retired from calling boxing matches in protest that the fight wasn't stopped sooner.

When Tex and I went at it in the river for our big fight scene, he was really hitting me—pounding and pounding my upper body in an exhausting series of takes. The man was a professional boxer, and the blows he landed were solid. I didn't want to look like a wimp, but I finally had to speak up.

"Tex," I said, "I know you're supposed to kick my ass in this scene, but you've got to back off a little bit here."

"What's the matter, Little Buddy?" he spat back. "You can't take it? Is it too much for you?" I liked Tex, but the sneer on his face as he taunted me was too much. And when he started pounding on me again, finally knocking me down hard in the river, I lost it.

Tex had punched me hard enough to spin me around and put me on my hands and knees in the river. I got up slowly, and without looking at him I took a hitch step backward, went one running step, and hit him square in the face—harder than I'd ever hit anyone in my life. The blow rocked his head back, and when it came forward again I saw that he had a big old smile on his face. And then he laughed.

"Is that all you've got, Little Buddy?" Tex said, chuckling. I just stared at him in disbelief. I'd hit him with all my strength, and he hadn't even felt the blow.

It was as if nothing could hurt Tex. As a result, he seemed to think nothing could hurt anyone else, either. One time, he was carrying an AK-47 loaded with blanks, but instead of handling it according to the set's safety rules, he aimed it right at my crotch and pulled the trigger. As he laughed maniacally, a burst of fire and smoke shot out, frying my pants and damn near turning me into a eunuch.

But as crazy as Tex was, he and I ended up becoming good buddies. Nobody else would share a dressing room with him because he was too much of a wild man, so I did for a while, until his partying ways got to be too much for me, too, and I pitched a tent for myself nearby. Tex loved Bangkok's red-light district, Patpong, and spent plenty of nights there—as did many of the other guys in the cast and crew, some of whom later had to be treated for gonorrhea. But only one guy decided to stay behind after we wrapped filming: Tex. He cashed in his plane ticket home, and the last we saw him, he was heading back to Patpong. We did eventually see him a couple more times over the years, but whenever I'd ask how he finally made it out of Thailand, he'd just say, "Little Buddy, you don't want to know."

*Uncommon Valor* was a good movie, for what it was. But I still wanted to find roles that would stretch me more as an actor. In *The Renegades, The Outsiders,* and *Uncommon Valor,* I played tough young guys who knew how to fight. The characters were different in many ways, but only in degree. And I was getting tired of playing characters younger than myself—I easily looked five or ten years younger than I was, so that's how I was always cast.

But after *Uncommon Valor,* I was cast in *Grandview, U.S.A.* for the role of Ernie "Slam" Webster, a Demolition Derby driver in a love triangle. Slam Webster had something of the wild child in him, too, but he was more mature than my other characters, making this the first time I was cast as a more mature man, rather than a young man. Tommy Howell was cast as Tim Pearson, my rival for the hand of Michelle "Mike" Cody, played by Jamie Lee Curtis.

Lisa worked on the film, too, choreographing a dream dance sequence—the first time she and I worked together on a movie. I was especially happy she was there because the town where we were shooting—Pontiac, Illinois—had only about ten thousand people, so there wasn't a hell of a lot to do. In fact, Pontiac's main claim to fame was its prison, which employed or incarcerated most of the people in town. Just about the only half-interesting place to go was the Courtyard Hotel, where the Teamsters and other movie crew stayed. We called it the Gorilla Villa.

Apart from getting drinks at Gorilla Villa there wasn't much to keep us occupied in Pontiac, so *Grandview* marked the beginning of what became a tradition for me: playing elaborate pranks on the set. I may have been cast in my first "adult" role, but off camera I was playing pranks like a big kid. And I didn't endear myself to the director, Randal Kleiser, with one I played on him.

One night, Lisa, Tommy Howell, and I had been invited over to the house where Randal was staying during the shoot. After we left, we got the bright idea of going back to sneak in, as we thought there might be something interesting going on with Jamie Lee Curtis. I can't even remember what we thought might be happening, but we were bored and probably tipsy, so we headed back over to Randal's place.

Lisa stayed in the car while Tommy and I found an open door and snuck upstairs. Jamie Lee wasn't there, but we did overhear Randal in a, shall we say, private moment with someone else—so we turned around and hightailed it back out. Randal must have heard us and realized who it was, because the next day on set he was pretty cool to me. Lisa was embarrassed, and although Randal didn't hold it against her, he did later make reference to the fact that she'd driven the "getaway car."

But that prank paled in comparison to the ones pulled on my next movie, *Red Dawn*. In fact, everything on *Red Dawn* was epic in scale: the hard-core training, the controversial plot, the insanely rigorous shoot, and the antagonism between myself and a certain young actress—one who would later dance with me in the movie that shot us both to stardom.

# Chapter 7

Y ou can call me the General," *Red Dawn* director John Milius announced. "Swayze, you are my Lieutenant of the Art, and I'll direct these little fuckers through you." With those words, Milius put me in charge of the cast of *Red Dawn*— Tommy Howell, Jennifer Grey, Charlie Sheen, Lea Thompson, and others—for the grueling shoot in the mountains of New Mexico.

*Red Dawn* was a controversial movie right from the start. Five minutes into the film, Soviet and Cuban paratroopers float down to a small Colorado town and open fire with machine guns, launching World War III with an invasion on American soil. In the early 1980s, when we made *Red Dawn*, the Cold War was raging and fears of a Soviet attack ran high across America. But nobody would touch it as a movie plot— except Milius, who was just the man for the job.

Milius was a wild man and a military freak. He had a collection of firearms and an encyclopedic knowledge of arms and armaments, and he even kept a loaded gun on his desk at the 20th Century Fox offices. Milius wrote *Apocalypse Now* and cowrote *Dirty Harry,* and he loved war games. He consulted military experts while cowriting *Red Dawn*, even reportedly asking former secretary of state Alexander Haig for help. Milius wanted *Red Dawn* to be as realistic as possible, so he started with training his cast as if we were really a band of scared teenage soldiers, rather than actors on a movie set.

I played Jed Eckert, the leader of a group of high school students who manage to escape to nearby wooded mountains after the Soviet invasion. The movie follows our group—dubbed the Wolverines, after the local high school mascot—as we survive a freezing winter, foraging for food and skirmishing with Russian soldiers who track us down. To prepare us for our roles, Milius arranged for real mercenaries to train us in military tactics, after which we'd take part in real war games with a National Guard unit before filming.

The mercenaries taught us all about military maneuvers and survival techniques. We fired weapons, learned how to camouflage ourselves, and undertook stealth maneuvers through the woods. It was dirty, tiring, and physically demanding—and I loved every minute of it. When our training culminated in a giant game of Capture the Flag, with the ragtag Wolverines going up against the National Guard troops, I wanted more than just to show off what we'd learned. I wanted to capture that flag and win.

Our objective was to start from the cover of a forested mountainside, cross an open valley, and take the flag planted on the other side of the valley. We had three days to do it, with hundreds of trained National Guardsmen trying to stop us.

From the moment we set up camp on that mountainside, I became Jed Eckert. Right away, this game became a matter of life and death—I almost felt like my life really did depend on capturing that flag. And I treated the other Wolverines that way, too, yelling and pushing them to their absolute limits in the game. Charlie Sheen and Tommy Howell loved it—they were as gung ho as I was. But Lea Thompson and Jennifer Grey seemed taken aback at my intensity. In fact, it's probably safe to say Jennifer couldn't stand me once I started barking orders at everyone.

Getting across the open valley was going to be tricky, and I doubt the seasoned National Guard troops expected much from us. But we had a plan. With the help of some crew members, we dug a network of shallow trenches and camouflaged them as best we could. Once they were covered with plywood and dirt and sod, you could even step on them in some spots without realizing anyone was underneath. In fact, during our assault across the valley, which took place at night, one National Guardsman almost stepped right on my face—and he never even knew I was there.

When we captured the flag after our all-night valley crossing, the National Guard troops were stunned—and pissed off. Milius, on the other hand, was elated and couldn't wait to start shooting. He had his real Wolverines. We had bonded out there in the trenches, and we had transformed into a pack of high school mujahideen, just like he wanted.

The hard part was that once I became Jed Eckert, I didn't ever want to step out of character. I really became this mercenary warrior, this almost-savage kid-turned-military-leader. When Lisa came out to the set, she couldn't reach me—I was afraid to just be Patrick again, fearing that if I dropped the character,

I wouldn't be able to get him back. It was frustrating for Lisa, and yet I couldn't stop. This was a huge role for me—my first real leading role in a big Hollywood film—and I had to nail it.

The film's setting added to the realism. We shot in the area around Las Vegas, New Mexico, which had its own rough-and-tumble reputation. A hundred years ago, Las Vegas was the last point on the Santa Fe Trail to get supplies, get drunk, and get laid before heading into the Rockies to die in your wagon train. It has always been a real tough-guy kind of town, and it wasn't the most welcoming place for random Anglos who ambled in.

This was especially true of the town's bars, which were the kind of places where the men carried knives and half of them got pulled out on any given night. Tommy, Charlie, and I would roll into bars just about every evening, sometimes staying until the sun came up.

One night, Charlie, Tommy, Brad Savage, and I went to a bar to play some pool—Charlie was a great player, and he was giving us some tips. I never knew what started it, but suddenly all hell broke loose and every guy in the bar was flailing around, punching, slashing with a knife, or breaking a bar stool over someone's head. Blood and beer were flying everywhere, and I looked at my guys and thought, "I gotta get them out of here!" Tommy and Brad were just kids, about eighteen years old, and I was Jed, their leader, responsible for getting them safely away from danger.

I grabbed a pool cue and broke it in half, then started swinging it around wildly, like a weapon. I just started whaling on whoever was in the way, trying to make an opening for us. Charlie, Tommy, and Brad pushed in behind me, shoving and punching all the way, and we finally got to the front door, where I threw down the bloody pool cue and we took off. The Wolverines had escaped the enemy again!

The funny thing was, Lisa and I ended up buying a ranch in that same area years later. And when we brought up those bar fights with a few locals, they remembered them. Apparently these were some of the biggest brawls in the history of Las Vegas, New Mexico. And they'll probably never be topped now, because the town's seediest bars have all gradually disappeared in the years since *Red Dawn*. It's now a quaint, friendly historical town with a colorful past.

Despite the movie's dead-serious theme—or maybe because of it—the pranks we played on the set were epic. *Red Dawn* was a violent war movie, with hundreds of explosions from bombs, machine guns, missiles, and grenades, so the crew had every kind of explosive imaginable. And unlike some directors, Milius was as wild as the rest of us, so I aimed pranks at him as much as at anyone.

One time, I rigged the toilet in his trailer with charges—M60s, which are like one-eighth-size sticks of dynamite. I packed them into a steel tube to direct the force, so they wouldn't blow shrapnel everywhere, and taped them under his toilet. When Milius went in to do his business, I detonated them—and the explosion sent him running out the door in a panic. He'd barely gotten the words "Swayze, you son of a—" out of his mouth when I set off a second round of explosives, blowing two garbage cans sky-high and scaring the shit out of him.

Another time, I hid a bottle-rocket launcher in his room. I packed a few dozen little bottle rockets into a rack I'd made and rigged it to go off when Milius tried to open his door in the morning. Sure enough, when he pushed the door open the next morning, dozens of tiny rockets flew at him, driving him back into his room. Day to day, he never knew what might be coming at him—and he loved it.

Milius loved explosives, and he'd gone to amazing lengths to make sure everything on *Red Dawn* was authentic. I still get chills when I think about the scene where the paratroopers float out of the sky, landing on the field next to the high school and then opening fire with machine guns. All the helicopters, tanks, airplanes, and missile launchers were absolutely true to the era, which lent an air of authenticity to the whole film. Watching it today, you can still feel the fear that was so rampant throughout the Cold War.

The realism was also aided by the fact that we really did camp out during what became the coldest winter in years, with temperatures plunging at times to thirty below. My fingers became frostbitten from all the hours spent in the elements, and to this day they throb painfully whenever it's cold. We really became those characters—scanning the skies for helicopters, rationing our food, riding horses across the mountains. And we even had to perform our own heroics when a freak accident nearly led to disaster one afternoon.

The actors playing the Wolverines were riding in a van, which was towing a horse trailer behind it. The mountain road was steep, icy, and treacherous, with a sheer dropoff to one side. As we towed the horse trailer up the road, it began sliding on the ice, right toward the edge of the cliff. The trailer slid to a wobbly stop just on the edge of this massive drop. If it went a yard or two farther, it would go down—and pull the van and us right over with it.

Everybody in the van was completely freaked out, but Tommy Howell and I jumped into action. "Get in the doorway!" I yelled. "Don't get out of the van, because that'll send the trailer over. But get in the doorway so you can jump if it starts to go anyway!"

While everyone crowded into the van's doorway, Tommy and I jumped out to deal with the horses. There was a gap between the road and the horse trailer's door, so we'd have to get the horses to jump across the gap to safety. The problem was, the horses were going crazy with fear. We gingerly made our way out to the trailer, unlatched the gate, and guided the horses one by one to the road, urging them to jump across the gap. Somehow, we managed to get them all to safety—and once the horses were out of the trailer, it was light enough for the van to pull it back up to the road. Tommy and I were as elated as if we'd single-handedly repelled a Soviet air attack, and we high-fived each other while the other actors breathed sighs of relief.

I loved playing Jed Eckert, and I enjoyed every minute of being the leader of our ragtag band, even if it was a little intense for others. As I mentioned, Jennifer Grey was probably the least impressed of all—she really chafed when I ordered her around, and rolled her eyes when I stayed in character between takes. But there was a moment at the end of the film when Jennifer seemed to warm to me. It was when we shot her character's death scene.

Jennifer's character, Toni, has been mortally wounded following a Soviet aerial attack, but Jed doesn't want to let her die. In that scene, I scoop her up onto the back of my horse and flee the attack, but it's too late for her. Toni and Jed end up taking refuge under a piñon tree, and she asks Jed to finish her off with a pistol. But he can't.

It's a very tender scene, and as I stroked Jennifer's hair, it was a genuinely emotional moment. This was the first time she and I had a meaningful scene together, and I think it endeared me to her after all the friction we had. The funny thing is, most of that scene ended up being cut. But even in the shorter version that made it into the film, it was clear to anyone watching that Jennifer and I had chemistry together.

*Red Dawn* came out in the summer of 1984, just as Lisa and I were starring together in a very different kind of performance. In fact, *Without a Word* was just about as far as you could get from the freezing Cold War drama of *Red Dawn*. It was an intimate, deeply emotional reflection on dancing, dreams, and what happens when those dreams die.

It had all started months earlier, when Lisa and I danced in a special performance for our acting class. We were studying with Milton Katselas, a legendary acting coach in LA. We had waited years to get into his class, but it was well worth it. Milton pushed us further, and made us dig deeper, than ever before.

We weren't the only dancers in Milton's class—in fact, it wasn't unusual for former ballet dancers to turn to acting once they left the profession full-time. But one thing we noticed was that all these former dancers felt like we did, that nothing really filled the void left by dancing. Lisa and I became close to one in particular, an amazingly talented former Paul Taylor Company dancer named Nicholas Gunn. We'd hang out together after class, sitting at diners and talking about the passion and pain of dancing, and how we'd drop everything in a heartbeat for the chance to do it all again.

These were little more than idle conversations until we were invited to dance for a special scene in acting class. There was a cellist in the class who was also studying acting, and he wanted to explore different forms of expression through music. He asked Nicholas, Lisa and me, and another dancer and actress named Shanna Reed to perform dance pieces while he played, with the class watching.

For our part, Lisa and I prepared a pas de deux. And the feeling I got while being onstage, dancing ballet once again, was far more intense than I had expected. I felt my heart swell in my chest as Lisa and I moved together, with the gentle moan of the cello guiding us. It had been so long since I had danced in front of others, and so long since I'd felt that amazing soaring in my spirit. It was beautiful, and painful, and in the end, devastating. No matter how much success I had begun to have in the acting world, nothing compared to the sheer exhilaration of dancing.

When the performance ended, Lisa and I went backstage and I just broke down sobbing. I was overwhelmed with feelings—all the feelings I'd buried when I had to leave Eliot Feld. I had forced myself to cope after leaving Eliot Feld, because I had to. My dream had been shattered, but I couldn't let that shatter my life. What I now realized, weeping backstage at the Beverly Hills Playhouse, was that I had a lot of emotional unfinished business related to leaving the ballet.

Lisa and Nicholas felt the same way I did, so we resolved to do something about it. It was time to explore all those feelings, to truly give them voice. And Milton Katselas offered a vehicle for us to do it. He had started a program called Camelot Productions, which offered free space for people who wanted to develop new plays. We could write about all these pent-up emotions, create a combination drama and dance work, and produce it at Camelot.

Lisa, Nicholas, and I got right to work, coming up with ideas and scenes through improvisations. Lisa would write all our ideas down and shape them, and we worked to make seamless transitions between talking and dancing. We wanted the dancing to say as much as the dialogue and monologues, which eventually led to our title: *Without a Word.*

The centerpiece was three monologues, one each by Lisa, Nicholas, and me. We wanted to express our innermost thoughts and feelings about dance, making the piece extremely personal. The day we decided to create these monologues, Lisa went home and started writing furiously. She was so driven and focused, she wrote the entire thing in one night and set it to music. And the next day, when she read her completed, beautiful monologue to Nicholas and me, we just looked at each other. Nicholas said, "Well, she's certainly set the bar high."

Doing *Without a Word* was both frightening and exhilarating for me. One of the most important themes in my life is learning how to seek out another dream when one dies. Too many people get swallowed by disappointment when their dream doesn't work out, and I had always made sure I wasn't one of those people. But now I was digging back into that disappointment—poking and exploring it. The result was a tremendous outpouring of emotion. A catharsis.

We put on three preview performances of *Without a Word* in the summer of 1984, then reworked it for a month-long run at the Beverly Hills Playhouse that fall. Every single show sold out, and audiences left the theater in tears. A Who's Who of Hollywood stars came to see it, including Liza Minnelli, Drew Barrymore, and Melissa Gilbert in just one night. Gene Kelly came to a performance, too, and he particularly loved Lisa, whom he confessed to finding "very attractive." He and Liza pressed Lisa and me to take *Without a Word* to New York or make a movie of it, and separately, Gene encouraged me to pursue more musical venues. Apart from Gregory Hines, there just weren't that many male actors out there who could sing, dance, and act.

When all was said and done, we received six LA Drama Critics Awards, including Best Play, Best Direction, Best Actress for Lisa, and Best Actor for me. As an artistic endeavor, it was an amazingly satisfying experience. But that wasn't the best thing about it.

The best thing about the play was the response we got, and continued to get even years later, from people who'd seen it. For years, people would come up to Lisa or me and say, "I saw *Without a Word,* and it just moved me so much." They'd tell us about the dreams they'd had, and how they'd fallen by the wayside—until seeing our play. People were actually choosing to go back and follow their bliss, encouraged by what they'd seen onstage.

*Without a Word* touched a deep emotional chord in so many people, and it also cauterized wounds for both Lisa and me. Of all the endeavors we've undertaken, we both remember *Without a Word* as one of our proudest artistic moments.

By the time *Without a Word* premiered, Lisa and I had been together ten years. We'd been through a lot in that time: the untimely end of our ballet careers, moving across the country, going broke, my dad's death, my foray into too much drinking. But through it all, I still felt a magic with her, which our emotional work together on *Without a Word* confirmed.

In the decade we'd been together, I had seen Lisa grow from a naïve eighteen-year-old into a confident woman. She wasn't afraid of anything, and jumped right into whatever we got ourselves into, from woodworking to acting to playwriting. Lisa was game for everything, and she never lost her sense of humor even in the hard times. The longer we were together, the luckier I felt that we'd found each other. And I even began to let myself believe she wanted to be with me, too.

One reason we fit so well together was that we shared so many interests. We both loved dancing, acting, traveling, being out in nature. We also both loved horses, and even shared a dream of possibly owning a few someday. But when we finally took the first step toward that dream, it was more like a funny misstep.

While we were on the set of *Red Dawn,* both Lisa and I had fallen in love with a horse in the movie named Fancy. As shooting was winding down, I asked the movie's horse wrangler if he'd sell Fancy to us. We still lived in an apartment, so we couldn't keep him at home, but we figured he could live at the equestrian-center stables in LA. Fancy was a gorgeous, high-stepping Morgan parade horse, with his head always jacked up so high that sitting on him was like sitting on the back of a seahorse.

I offered the wrangler $150, hoping it would be enough. To my relief, he agreed. He led Fancy out of a trailer and held out the lead rope. "He's all yours!" he said.

I'd just bought a horse! What was I going to do with him now? I took the rope and began to lead Fancy away, and at that very moment one of the old ranch hands was walking by.

"This is my new horse!" I said, a big smile on my face.

"That horse is lame," the old-timer replied. He pointed at

Fancy's legs, and I was forced to admit what I'd noticed earlier but tried to ignore. Fancy had a slight limp in his right rear leg. We'd bought a lame horse, with bowed tendons, but I loved him anyway—he and I had been through that freezing winter together. And despite his limp, Fancy still turned out to be a great first horse for us.

Being the son of a cowboy, I had grown up with horses and loved them all my life. Our family didn't have much money, but horses were cheap in Texas, so we kept a few at some run-down stables near our house. We'd barter with the stable owners, exchanging chores for boarding, so from the time I was small, I learned how to muck stalls and care for horses. And because those corrals were so ratty, the horses needed a lot of attention, for things like splinters and hoof injuries.

We even had an Arabian mare when I was growing up. She wasn't necessarily well-bred, but she was an Arabian, and we bred her to have a foal, whom we named Princess Zubidiya of Damascus. We called her Zubi. I loved that horse more than anything when I was a boy, and rode her every chance I got. And I learned horsemanship from a master—my dad.

My dad was absolutely beautiful in the saddle. He was like John Wayne. He'd been riding since he could walk, and he came from a long line of cowboys. His father—my grandfather—had been a foreman at the King Ranch in Texas, which at 825,000 acres was the size of Rhode Island, and one of the biggest ranches in the world. My grandfather was shot to death by cattle rustlers before my dad was born, and according to family lore, the killers sat there smoking his cigarettes while they waited for him to die.

My grandmother remarried after that, and my step-grandfather was a cowboy, too, up in the Texas Panhandle.

When I was growing up, I used to go there in the summers and work with him on the ranch. His name was Cap, but we kids called him Pe-Paw, which he hated. Later, when we'd go into bars together, he'd say, "Little Buddy, you call me Cap in this bar, don't be calling me that piece of shit Pe-Paw!" I loved him to death, but of course I'd call him Pe-Paw just to drive him crazy.

These were the men who passed on to my dad—and me—the cowboy way. Even though I moved to New York and LA, becoming a dancer and an actor, I never lost that cowboy blood. My dad and I used to talk about owning a ranch together someday, with a stable of horses and big outdoor spaces. He died before I could make it happen for us, but I kept that dream alive and swore to myself that Lisa and I would buy a beautiful ranch in his honor when we had the money.

In late 1984, five years after moving to Los Angeles, I finally got the role that would enable me to buy a small ranch and start moving back into the cowboy life. And ironically enough, I'd be playing a man who spent much of his own life on horseback.

# Chapter 8

O rry Main, the swashbuckling Confederate Army soldier in *North and South,* was the role that sent my career soaring. A twelve-hour miniseries based on the extremely popular John Jakes historical novels, *North and South* was a TV event that rivaled the epic *Roots* miniseries of the late 1970s.

The story revolved around the Confederate Orry and his Union soldier friend George Hazard, played by Jim Read. Orry and George meet at West Point, and the miniseries follows their friendship through the tumult of the Civil War and beyond. *North and South* was a huge undertaking, with more than 130 cast members, thousands of extras, nearly nine thousand wardrobe pieces, and fifteen thousand props and set decorations being trucked to different locations all over the South. It was a certifiable Big TV Event.

I was incredibly excited to win the role of Orry, and not just because he was the kind of Renaissance-man, courageous southern gentleman I'd always aspired to be. Playing Orry meant that I'd be starring alongside the most amazing cast ever assembled for a television series. Elizabeth Taylor, James Stewart, Olivia de Havilland, Johnny Cash, David Carradine,

Lesley-Anne Down, Gene Kelly, Robert Mitchum, Jean Sim-
mons, Kirstie Alley, Lloyd Bridges, and Waylon Jennings all
had parts in *North and South*—and that's just a partial list.

As they say in football, when you score a touchdown, you
should try to act like you've been in the end zone before. So I
was determined that, even though I'd be playing opposite
some of the greatest actors of all time, I'd try to be cool about
it. I especially tried to remember this the day I was scheduled
to do a scene with James Stewart.

It was early in the shoot, so I hadn't done many scenes with
the big stars yet. Because Jim Read and I were the leads of the
series, I wanted to project confidence. But when I heard James
Stewart's distinctive voice as I walked toward the set for our
scene, my knees turned to jelly. And when I saw him sitting
behind an ornate desk, in character as Miles Colbert, I couldn't
believe I'd been lucky enough to be cast opposite Hollywood
legends like him. For a young actor, it was the opportunity of
a lifetime.

In addition to feeling incredibly lucky to be on that set, I
also loved everything about my role. *North and South* was set in
a time when men were men and women were women, and the
courtliness and southern gentility of the time really appealed
to my old-fashioned side. I loved walking down the streets on
the set, seeing the men in their military uniforms and the
women in their corsets and gowns, their cleavage spilling out
as they fanned themselves in the heat.

The set even came equipped with "leaning boards," as
women couldn't sit down in their giant ball-gown dresses without crushing all that crinoline. Instead, they'd prop themselves gently against the leaning board, resting their lower
backs and legs without sitting. Walking by a row of corseted

beauties, dressed in my sharp Confederate Army uniform, I felt like I'd gone back in time.

We filmed all over the South, in Mississippi, Arkansas, Louisiana, South Carolina, Texas. And because we were making not only the twelve-hour *North and South,* but also *North and South: Book II,* we ended up shooting for a year and a half. It was amazing to have that much guaranteed work, at a really good salary. Even on *The Outsiders,* which was not only a Francis Ford Coppola movie but also did very well at the box office, I'd received only scale pay. It was worth it, of course, to work with Coppola. But both Lisa and I were really happy to finally have some real money coming in during *North and South.*

I felt like I earned it, though, considering how intense the shooting schedule and conditions were. We shot six days a week, for no less than twelve hours a day. And some of the longest days were right in the middle of the South Carolina summer, when we'd sometimes spend up to eighteen hours shooting, wearing those heavy woolen uniforms. I even fainted once on the set, slamming my face into a cement column and breaking my nose before hitting the ground. But when Jim Read and I asked permission to take our coats off for one scene on a train, director Richard T. Heffron first had to confirm with a Civil War expert that it would be historically accurate before he said yes.

The producers did absolutely everything they could to ensure historical authenticity. Some of the costumes were made with nineteenth-century silk, and others were borrowed from actual historical collections or made from period drawings. The best source of costumes, however, was the hundreds of Civil War re-enactors who played in the battle scenes.

This was my first time meeting hard-core re-enactors, and I

was amazed at how particular they were about everything. When they were re-enacting a battle, they not only wore clothes that were true to the period, even down to their underwear, but they also didn't eat any food or use any tools or weapons that weren't available during the Civil War. These re-enactors, some of whom were descendants of soldiers who had fought in the battles we re-created, looked as if they had walked in through a time machine.

The cast also had several different coaches, to help ensure we stayed in character. Our dialect coach, Robert Easton, made sure everyone spoke with the proper drawl or brogue, and dance historian Desmond Strobel taught us how to dance an authentic "Sicilian Circle" and "Lancers Quadrille." The result of all this attention to detail was a miniseries that looked, sounded, and felt like a real Civil War setting.

Depending on the cast and the general mood, film and TV sets can be pretty wild places. On *Red Dawn*, we'd gotten into some crazy pranks, partly to defuse the tension of the shoot, which was both physically grueling and emotionally draining. But on *North and South*, the cast wasn't into pranks so much as having a good time. It was a fun group, and Lisa and I loved hanging out with everyone in the evenings after shooting.

We did a lot of filming in Charleston, South Carolina, which is packed with fantastic restaurants in its tree-lined, beautifully preserved old section of town. One restaurant in particular, Philippe Million's, became a cast hangout. We'd head there nearly every weekend, ordering drinks and enjoying the kitchen's nouvelle cuisine. Some actors could be found there several times a week, including Lesley-Anne Down, who we'd heard had her own reasons for wanting to spend as much time as possible in expensive restaurants.

Lesley, who played my love interest, Madeline Fabray, in the series, had already starred in countless TV shows and films, including *The Pink Panther Strikes Again* and the BBC's popular *Upstairs, Downstairs*. At the time we were shooting *North and South,* she and her then-husband, the director Billy Friedkin, were heading toward a bitter divorce. And it seemed to some in the cast that Lesley was aiming to spend as much of Billy's money as she could before it was final.

So on the nights she was at Philippe Million's, the Cristal was flowing and the food kept coming—courtesy of Lesley and, unbeknownst to him, Billy. She must have spent tens of thousands of dollars at that restaurant, to the delight of the rest of the cast. We'd all eat and drink to our hearts' content, then head out the door to a nearby place to dance. It was a pretty lively group, and there were a lot of late nights.

Lesley also treated herself to an upgrade over the cast housing in Charleston, which was already nothing to sneeze at. She upgraded to a penthouse suite, which she paid for with her own money. And she was generous with that, too, inviting us all up a couple of times for drinks in her suite, with its fantastic view of Charleston.

On one of those evenings, a whole group gathered in Lesley's suite and continued to party late into the night. The last thing I remembered was talking with David Carradine, and the next thing I knew, I was waking up the next morning in my hotel room slightly hung over. But the next afternoon, Lesley said to me, "Patrick, I was so worried about you last night!"

"Why?" I asked.

"Well," she said in her clipped British diction, "you and

David were out on that tiny ledge, outside the window, doing karate with bottles of Crown Royal in your hand. I was scared to death!"

I just stared at her. I had no recollection of going out on the ledge—why would I do a crazy thing like that? After all, her suite was up on the twelfth floor. But apparently, it was true. David was a big martial arts guy—he'd played the lead in the seventies TV series *Kung Fu*—and he and I had apparently gone out to the ledge to demonstrate our balance skills in Kata, a form of slow-motion shadow boxing. Thank goodness, even with alcohol in our bloodstreams, our balance was good enough to keep from tumbling to the beautiful cobblestones of Charleston twelve floors below.

Needless to say, Lisa wasn't in Charleston with us that particular weekend. Otherwise, I wouldn't have been out there on the ledge in the first place. I definitely tended toward more drinking and late nights when she wasn't with me—I never have been able to stand the inside of a hotel room alone. When I was missing Lisa, I just wanted the nights to go by faster, and staying out was my admittedly imperfect way of trying to make that happen.

The wild energy running through that whole shoot also included hookups among cast and crew. Lesley-Anne Down ended up in a relationship with the cinematographer, Don FauntLe-Roy, and the two have been together ever since. Jim Read got together with Wendy Kilbourne. And Genie Francis, of *General Hospital* fame, started dating actor Jonathan Frakes, whom she married a few years later. It was certainly never boring on the set of *North and South*, either during filming or after hours.

But as much as I loved my fellow cast members on *North and South*, I probably loved the horses even more. There were some gorgeous horses on that set, including John Wayne's last horse, Parsons. Parsons and I had an amazing connection—it was almost telepathic. All I had to do was think about what I wanted him to do next, and he'd do it.

There were plenty of good horse scenes in both parts of *North and South,* but the best one came in *Book II.* Orry, who's now a general, is riding away from camp with two of his aides, when suddenly the camp comes under attack. The three of us have to turn around and come to the rescue, with guns blazing.

Just before we shot the scene, I had an idea. I was always trying to figure out ways to make the action scenes more exciting, and I knew I'd hit on something great with this: We should hold the horses' reins in our teeth, so we could fire rifles with both hands as we raced through the battle.

The two guys who played my aides were hard-core, badass re-enactors. They had the long hair and grizzled look of real Civil War soldiers, and this was how they spent their leisure time—traveling around the country, putting on re-enactments, and handing down knowledge of the Civil War era to future generations. These were real manly men, with full beards, powerful builds, and leathery skin. I just knew they'd be ready to up the ante on this scene.

We were all three astride our horses, and just as the director was about to yell, "Action!" I said to the two guys, "Hey, dudes— we've got these double-barreled short shotguns; let's ride with the reins in our teeth so we can fire with both hands!"

The guys just shook their heads.

"Come on!" I said. "It'll be cool!"

They shook their heads again. "No way," said one of the guys, sitting back in his saddle.

"Well, why not?" I asked, exasperated. We had a chance to make this scene really pop, and these guys wouldn't even consider it.

"Teeth," the guy finally said. And he reached up and popped his front teeth right out of his mouth. It took me a second to realize it was a denture.

"Oh, shit," I said. "How'd that happen?"

"Riding with the reins in my teeth," the guy replied, and calmly placed the bridge back in his mouth. "If that horse trips, it'll knock your teeth right out of your head."

Just then the director yelled, "Action!" We all took off, and despite the warning, I held the reins in my teeth for the whole shot. I kept my back as rubbery as possible, trying to absorb every little jolt with anything but my teeth. But I didn't need to worry, because Parsons was such a good, sure-footed horse that he raced silkily around every obstacle, including the dozens of soldiers' "corpses" on the ground. The shot turned out amazing, and fortunately all my teeth stayed in my head.

The first installment of *North and South* aired in November 1985, and suddenly Jim Read and I found our faces plastered all over newspapers, magazines, billboards, and TV shows.

ABC had ratcheted up its publicity machine, and that, combined with Americans' enduring interest in the Civil War, turned the miniseries into a huge TV event. The television landscape wasn't so fragmented in the 1980s as it is now, with hundreds of cable channels, DVRs, and the internet competing for attention, so millions of people tuned in to see the installments as they aired.

The floodgates were officially open. Patrick Swayze fan clubs started appearing and interview requests were pouring in. Now, whenever we went out in public, Lisa and I would find ourselves surrounded. Before *North and South,* people might recognize me on the street and ask for an autograph. But after the miniseries aired, fans were suddenly everywhere, approaching us on all sides no matter where we were. I have to admit, it was kind of cool.

But as the level of fame went up, the level of courtesy sometimes went down. People would interrupt a conversation, cut someone off, or even jump in front of our car to ask for an autograph. And when we went to events, the organizers would often take my arm and try to lead me away, completely ignoring the fact that Lisa was with me. In those cases, I'd interject loudly, "Have you met my wife, Lisa?" and they'd get the picture. But it wasn't always easy for us to be polite in the face of the increasing whirlwind surrounding us.

Yet we've always tried to accommodate fans' requests for autographs, photos, or anything else. After all, Lisa and I both know we wouldn't be where we are if it weren't for the fans, and we're incredibly appreciative of all the support they've given us over the years. For the most part, people are very nice even when they're asking for something, so it's easy to be nice back. And of course, I'm the kind of guy who always wants people to like me, so I have extra motivation for being nice to those who approach us.

Lisa has always taken the attention in stride, even when women fans get a little more aggressive. She's not the jealous type, for one thing. And besides, she knows as well as anyone that all the attention is good for my career.

Just after *North and South* aired, Lisa was talking to an actress friend of ours named Barb, who worked as an office temp when she was between roles. Barb had just spent the day at an office building in LA, and she was concerned about what she'd been hearing at the water cooler. "Lisa," she said, "there's a girl in this office who's obsessed with Patrick. She kept saying she was going to find a way to meet him, that she wanted him and was going to find a way to get him!" Barb was seriously trying to warn her, but Lisa just laughed.

"Barb," she said, "that's great! This is a good thing! This is just what we need." Barb couldn't quite believe it, but that's been Lisa's attitude throughout my whole career.

But even though we were happy about my career taking off, we had to deal with some difficult situations after *North and South*. For one thing, my manager, Bob LeMond, who'd brought us out to LA and helped us get started, died of complications from AIDS. Bob had been a real mentor and friend, and we'd known him since our days in Houston. Losing him at this point in my career, just three years after my father died, was devastating.

Lisa and I also realized that we'd now have to take steps to protect our privacy. Even in those pre-internet days, there were still paparazzi all over Hollywood, not to mention some overzealous fans who weren't above staking us out at home. When I got the role of Orry Main, it allowed us to buy a five-acre ranch, where we could keep horses and enjoy nature without being disturbed.

Yet although Lisa and I saw the potential for a dream home on our new property, when others saw it they were shocked. They thought we'd just bought ourselves a nightmare.

• • •

Nestled in the foothills of the San Gabriel Mountains about twenty miles north of Hollywood, the piece of land Lisa and I fell in love with was just a weed-choked lot when we bought it.

Used-car parts sat rusting, tumbleweeds blew through, and dead tree limbs and river rocks lay scattered across the property. The house wasn't even really a house—it was a couple of run-down cabins connected by a breezeway. The floors needed finishing, the kitchen needed renovating, the walls were made of plywood, and everything was generally a mess. But right from the start, it looked like heaven to us.

Ever since our first days of doing carpentry back in New York, Lisa and I felt ready to take on any project, no matter how large or small. This would be a very big project, but when we looked at those cabins and that land, we didn't see work and toil. We saw the potential for what this place could be. Lisa and I both had plenty of ideas, and we couldn't wait to get to work making them a reality.

We knew we'd need help, so the first thing we did was make it fun for friends to come out and join in the labor with us. We built the pool first, even before fixing up the house, so everybody who came out and sweated with us could have a nice cool dip afterward.

We invited friends to "rock parties" that had nothing to do with music: We'd fan people out across the property to pick up the rocks strewn everywhere, then have a big barbecue for everyone afterward. And a couple of times, we turned weed-cutting from a boring chore into a swordfighting lesson. I outfitted everyone with sabers and we all thrust and parried into the weeds, theatrically spinning and attacking our common foe. It was during one of these cleanup sessions that one of our friends gave our new home its name: Rancho Bizarro.

It was incredibly liberating to be out in nature again after all our years of living in LA and New York. Our ranch adjoins the Angeles National Forest, which made it feel as if our little five-acre spread was really a million-acre spread—we could ride horses deep into the wilderness, literally right outside our back door. The air was fresh and the smell of sage and oak permeated everything.

For the year when we were renovating, we lived in one of the small rooms and made tea and coffee on a little propane stove. We worked on the ranch every chance we got, creating a beautiful kitchen with terracotta floors and refinishing the wood floors ourselves—which Lisa says she'll never do again. We got to add our own special touches to the place, which made it that much more meaningful for us. Over time, we built trellised patios, a master-bedroom wing, a music studio, a dance studio, a guesthouse, and an office.

We also built a sixteen-stall pinewood barn, because living on the ranch wasn't just about fresh air and privacy. It was also about reclaiming the cowboy life. The smell of dirt and horse sweat and the raw masculine power of working on horseback was energizing for me, and I wanted to get back into it.

Lisa and I were lucky enough to know someone who could help us get fantastic horses. Gene McLaughlin was a world-champion trick roper, and his son Cliff had been a stunt double in *North and South*. To make ends meet between rodeos and trick-roping shows, Gene would buy horses down South and truck them to Los Angeles in a trailer, where he could sell each one for three to five times what he'd paid. We bought our second horse from him—a fantastic, talented horse named Cloud.

We called Cloud "Little Big Man," because he was small but rode big. Cloud and I would explore the mountains in the Angeles National Forest behind our ranch, sometimes going out for days at a time. I'd pack some food and water and a sleeping bag, and Cloud and I would just hit the trails. Some of my happiest memories of this time of my life were of Cloud and me exploring the deepest reaches of the woods together, miles from people and civilization. It always reminded me of being with my dad, to the point where our journeys together felt almost spiritual.

Cloud was also an excellent calf-roping horse. Calf roping is the hardest rodeo sport, in my opinion, as it's incredibly physical and requires lightning reflexes and excellent timing. You have to rope the running calf off your speeding horse, then use the horse's stopping to propel yourself forward. You land on your feet running, hit the calf, flank it in the air, and simultaneously grab the feet to lace with the pigging string in a nice bouquet.

The whole thing takes about two seconds, but one wrong move can result in injury to you, the horse, the calf, or all three. Gene trained me, and I was off to the races—I loved getting down in the dirt and honing my skills. And with Gene, Cliff, and my cowboy friend Tommy Howell all doing calf roping, it was a really fun time.

With the pinewood barn finished and plenty of room for more horses, Lisa and I started thinking about buying the most beautiful, regal animals of all: Arabians. Yet even with the money I'd made on *North and South,* we still weren't sure we could afford them.

Arabians are the steeds of the gods, and expensive to buy. Originally bred in the Middle East, they have a proud bearing and gorgeous bone structure, with arched necks and high tails. A particularly beautiful Arabian is the kind of horse that can make you gasp as it prances by. And not only are they stunning to look at, they're also smart, with boundless energy. Arabians aren't the easiest horses to train—I always joke that you have to be at least as smart as the horse—but the result is a real partnership between horse and rider.

I'd always wanted to own an Arabian, and Lisa and I were fortunate enough to know two of the best breeders in the country—or the world, for that matter—Tom and Rhita Mc-Nair. So we decided to stop by and see the McNairs at Glenlock Farms one week when we were in Houston visiting Lisa's family. We'd already told them we weren't sure we were ready to buy, when a horse named Ferouk suddenly came trotting out of his gate. Ferouk was a stunner, an impressive, powerful, well-trained Western Pleasure horse. This was our first serious look at the Arabian breed, so we asked Tom's opinion.

"This one's a winner," he told us. "You could win competitions with Ferouk." Looking at that horse, with his gliding stride and dark, intelligent eyes, we knew it was true.

Lisa and I wanted to own Arabians to learn more and improve our personal horsemanship, and we also wanted to show them competitively. Tom knew this, and Ferouk seemed to understand it, too. He looked at us with those big brown eyes as if to say, "You and me! Let's go!" We knew right then it would be hard to resist this horse. So we asked Tom how much it would cost to buy Ferouk—and his answer stunned us. It was a lot less than what we'd expected. As Tom knew, it was a price we really couldn't say no to.

Lisa and I looked at each other and broke into big smiles. Without even saying it, we both knew we were about to buy our first Arabian.

And that was how we began showing horses. We didn't know much about it, but being dancers, we picked up the physical nuances quickly. Your bearing and carriage have to be as impressive as the horse's, as the horse takes its cues from you. After taking her first lesson in how to show, Lisa entered a competition the very next day—and placed third. She was hooked.

Ferouk was a smart, savvy horse, and he and Lisa bonded right away. They spent hours together, each bettering the other's performance, and soon they were an amazing team. Lisa was a natural, and less than a year after we bought Ferouk, she took him all the way to the U.S. Nationals competition. She competed there with people who had been showing horses their whole lives, but that didn't intimidate her in the least. Lisa's skills were phenomenal, and she brought the best out in Ferouk. She placed in the top ten in the Nationals—an incredible achievement. And I went top five in Region 9, the most difficult region in the country.

We competed seriously for a while, traveling all across the United States for horse shows. People always seemed surprised that we did everything ourselves, from mucking out stalls to scrubbing down the horses to staying in the same Motel 6s our trainers stayed at. I suppose people expected a couple of prima donnas, but to us the whole point was to be one with the horse, and not to stand out. Both Lisa and I loved getting down and dirty, even if it sometimes led to a little bit of gawking from fans.

In fact, people sometimes couldn't believe it was really us

out there. I was entered in a regional competition one week-end, and was riding Ferouk around the ring. My hair was still long from *North and South,* and as I rode atop our beautiful horse, my hair flying out behind me, a guy turned to his wife and said, "That guy rides like he thinks he's Orry Main!"

Lisa overheard him, but she didn't say anything. When I got closer, she heard him murmur, "Wait a second. That *is* Orry Main!" Lisa just smiled.

Unfortunately, the more famous I got, the more difficult it was to compete in horse shows. Working with horses, like work-ing with ballerinas, teaches you that it's not about yourself. It's about bringing out the beauty and precision and perfection of your partner—in this case, your horse. But as fans began to realize that I was showing horses, they'd come out to the are-nas and sometimes hang over the rail, shouting, waving pho-tos for autographs, or even worse, taking flash photos right in my horse's face.

I ended up switching from riding horses to showing at hal-ter, where you have the horse at the end of a lead rope. You teach the horse to stand in a certain way, pulling up the head and neck, and then you run, leading the horse through paces meant to show off its conformation and movement. This worked out a little better, though eventually, after *Dirty Danc-ing,* I'd have to stop showing altogether. It just wasn't fair to the horse or to the other competitors.

As Lisa and I worked to get Rancho Bizarro in order, we ac-cumulated more and more animals. Soon we had dogs, cats, horses, peacocks, and a chicken house that produced quanti-ties of eggs. I loved being around animals and felt a connec-tion with them that I felt with only a few people. Whenever an animal was upset, I could talk it down and soothe it—and they could do the same for me. Surrounded by acres of gorgeous land and our growing menagerie of animals, we felt that the ranch was a true haven.

And we'd soon need that haven more than ever, as 1987 would mark the release of my biggest movie yet—and the start of the craziest period of our lives.

# Chapter 9

I read the script for *Dirty Dancing* one evening in our new house. Right away it filled me with emotion—but not the kind it was supposed to. I didn't like it. It seemed fluffy— nothing more than a summer-camp movie. Lisa read it, too, and she felt the same way.

But at the same time, we both could see the kernel of a great story in there. The ideas behind *Dirty Dancing* were fantastic. There were elements of class conflict, relationships, sexual awakening, family issues—it had a little bit of everything. And even though the screenplay was weak, with some work it could explore all those elements through a strong story filled with compelling characters.

Potential is a wonderful thing, but would the writer and director be open to rewrites? The next morning, as Lisa and I worked on remodeling our kitchen, we talked about how the script could be better. And despite our initial reservations, we began to get a little excited about it. I was scheduled to go in and read for the part of Johnny Castle, a role that seemed perfect for me. I wanted to win it, but I also wanted to find out if we could really turn this into a great movie or not.

One thing that attracted me to *Dirty Dancing* was the fact that Emile Ardolino would be directing. Emile didn't have a mile-long Hollywood resume, but he came from the dance world and had done award-winning work, including a televised presentation of "Baryshnikov at the White House" and a documentary about Jacques d'Amboise called *He Makes Me Feel Like Dancin'* that won an Academy Award. *Dirty Dancing* would be Emile's first feature film, but he was a class act and really knew dance. If anyone could pull this off, it was Emile.

But I still had reservations about going for the role of Johnny Castle, for one big reason. Even if the script could be vastly improved, I wasn't sure this movie was the right step to take in my career.

The response to *Skatetown, U.S.A.* had made it clear that I could have my pick of similar roles—and make a lot of money doing them. But it was also clear that if I did choose that route, I might never be able to escape it. I'd always be seen as a dancer-turned-actor, rather than an actor. So in the eight years that had passed since *Skatetown, U.S.A.*, I had purposefully avoided roles that involved dancing or had any kind of teen-idol flavor. I'd turned down that four-picture deal with Columbia that would have shot me to fame. I'd buried myself in acting classes. And I had been constantly on the lookout for parts that could stretch me as an actor.

Now, with *Dirty Dancing*, I had a choice. Should I stick to my guns and refuse to take a dancing movie? Or was this a different kind of movie, one that would allow me to dance but also to stretch myself as an actor? I was scared to say yes, scared I'd be undoing what I'd worked for the last eight years to build. But at the same time, both Lisa and I believed that *Dirty Dancing* had the potential to be wonderful.

So, after many conversations with Lisa, I made my decision: I would go for it, and give this role absolutely everything I had. If I was going to that place—the sexual, sensual dance role—I was going there 100 percent. I knew Johnny Castle had the potential to turn me into everything Hollywood seemed to want me to be, which was not necessarily what I wanted to be. But part of me was also excited about doing a dance movie— and of course, we now had house payments to make, too. So that afternoon I said to Lisa, "Okay, here we go." And off we went, for the ride of our lives.

The role of Johnny Castle wasn't mine for the taking. First I had to go in for a couple of auditions, one where I read, and one where Jennifer Grey and I danced together.

Whenever I read for auditions, I prefer to improvise rather than doing all the lines straight up. So for that first reading, I talked about growing up without much money in Houston, and how dance was a magical form of escape. The truth is, I really identified with Johnny. He was a blue-collar fighter whose soul was stirred by the beauty of dance. He was the kind of man who combined a tough exterior with a gentle soul—the kind of man my dad was, and the kind I was trying to be. In that first audition, I didn't act out Johnny. I *was* Johnny.

For the second audition, Jennifer Grey and I went in to dance for writer Eleanor Bergstein, choreographer Kenny Ortega, and Emile Ardolino. Eleanor was incredibly close to the material—she'd based it partly on her own experiences in the early 1960s, when she was a teenage girl called "Baby" dancing in the Catskills, and the movie was really a labor of love for her. So she was the one who jumped up to show Jennifer and me what she wanted us to do.

Eleanor put on some music and half-talked, half-danced us through what she wanted. I wasn't exactly sure what she was looking for, but I took Jennifer into my arms and decided to wing it. Jennifer and I had never danced together before, and she probably still thought of me as that half-crazed forest warrior from *Red Dawn*. But as I led her through a couple of steps, we soon found ourselves in a comfortable rhythm together.

I moved her around slowly at first, pulling her toward me and spinning her back out. I wanted her to feel confident in her dancing, enough to lose herself in it a little bit and not feel self-conscious. We looked each other in the eyes, and though she was a little bit giggly at first, she soon got more comfortable. We started doing more complex moves, and as we danced I decided she was lithe enough and balanced enough to try a lift.

Lisa was in the room, too, so we showed Jennifer how the lift would work. Lisa and I had done it so many times, we made it look effortless. I knew that if I was to lift Jennifer successfully, she'd have to feel confident in it—and after watching me lift Lisa a couple of times, she seemed ready.

It's not easy for a female dancer to execute her first lift. She's got to trust her male partner completely and give in to the momentum he sets for her. Otherwise, one or both partners can get hurt. Jennifer got up and took Lisa's place, and as we continued talking with Eleanor and Kenny, I just took her and gently pressed her over my head. I showed her I could control her completely—she could go forward, she could go back, but she would never tumble either way if she didn't make any sudden moves.

Jennifer did break position a couple of times, which was a natural reaction for someone who's never done lifts before. "Don't worry," I told her. "No matter what position you're in, I can put you down safely." The next time I lifted her, she posed beautifully, and I lowered her slowly to the ground, with our eyes locked on each other. It was a lovely moment, and very sexy. The room was absolutely silent—everyone was just staring at us.

Jennifer smiled when I put her down, and from that moment on, I knew we had it. We did a couple more sensual dance moves, and when the audition was over, Eleanor had made up her mind. As she told us later, at that point she felt that if they didn't get me for the role of Johnny, they didn't have a movie.

As perfect as the role of Johnny was for me, the role of Penny was equally perfect for Lisa. She auditioned for it, and wowed everyone. But ultimately, Cynthia Rhodes was cast as Penny. Cynthia was also a good choice, but what tipped the scales was the fact that she'd had a starring role in *Staying Alive,* with John Travolta. Cynthia had some momentum, and momentum sells in Hollywood.

What we didn't know, but found out much later, was that Eleanor expected me to insist on casting Lisa as a condition of getting me. But I really didn't think of myself as having that kind of power as an actor, so it never even occurred to me to ask. As Lisa now jokes, because she and Cynthia are both slender and blond, half the time people think it's her in the movie anyway.

Once I'd been cast as Johnny, Lisa and I started looking at how the script might be improved. Eleanor, Emile, and others were doing the same thing, so it was definitely a group effort, but I was as grateful as ever for Lisa's insights. Whether rewriting scripts or honing my performance, she and I have worked together on every movie I've ever done—she has an amazing ear for dialogue, a great sense of story, and knows how to zero in on performance. More important, she's absolutely truthful, even if it's something I don't want to hear. I always knew I could trust her completely—which became more and more important as time went by and my stature in Hollywood grew.

A lot of actors surround themselves with "yes-men." They like to be told that everything they're doing is great, as it helps boost their confidence. But I'm the opposite. I want to know what's weak, so I can work on improving it. Whenever we worked on a script or scene for a movie, we'd always play devil's advocate with each other, switching positions and thinking through every angle but Sunday. What does the writer intend here? What does the director see? Could the story have higher stakes? Is this how my character would react? Do these characters talk like real live flesh-and-bone human beings? Once you've gone through every possible scenario with a script, when you get back down to the words on the page you know right away what works and what doesn't.

That's how Lisa and I work together: We find the intention and emotional flow of a scene, and the words follow naturally. As the great director Elia Kazan once said, our character is often revealed by how we conceal our emotions, not how we show them. So, good writing has a lot do with how much your character conceals, rather than reveals. For example, it rips the audience's heart out to see somebody go to the ends of the earth not to cry—much more so than watching someone over-emoting, crying in their pretzels.

The draft of the script we'd read only hinted at deeper sociological and emotional currents, but we all knew that if we could just push the characters a little further, and explore them a little more deeply, we'd really have something. So everyone jumped right in, working day and night to tear apart things that weren't working and deepen the parts that were. Eleanor's script had strong bones, but now we were adding the flesh to them—and we'd continue doing so all the way through filming. And by the time we were done, we had a beautiful script.

Some of what Lisa and I suggested made it into the film, and some didn't. We inserted the fight scene between Johnny and the cad waiter, Robbie, to give Johnny the rougher edge his character needed. We wrote it so Johnny would stop before knocking the guy out, though, since he'd be wary of getting fired—something that had no doubt happened to him before. Lisa and I also stayed up the entire night before filming the final scene, where Johnny grabs the microphone in front of everyone at the resort, so we could rewrite his big speech. Sometimes we'd be working on new dialogue right up to shooting—and then continue fixing it between takes. We never stopped trying to make it better.

I felt all along that Johnny should ultimately end up with Penny, as they were so much alike and a more realistic couple than Johnny and Baby. That change got overruled, which was probably for the best. But when some on the set suggested I tone down the dancing with Penny early on, I put my foot down. They were worried that the dance scenes between Johnny and Penny were too sexy, that they would overshadow the later dance scenes between Johnny and Baby. I knew that wasn't true, based on my audition with Jennifer. There was no doubt we'd be able to create the heat—and we did.

We did a lot of rewriting for the big final scene, but one line that I absolutely hated ended up staying in. I could hardly even bring myself to say "Nobody puts Baby in a corner" in front of the cameras, it just sounded so corny. But later, seeing the finished film, I had to admit it worked. And of course, it became one of the most-quoted lines in the entire movie. I even quote a version of it myself these days, saying "Nobody puts Patrick's pancreas in a corner" when people ask how I'm doing.

Throughout the filming, we kept inserting little touches to help flesh out the characters and their relationships. There were times when Jennifer giggled uncontrollably, not as part of the script, but because she was just plain giggly—and those moments made it into the film. For the scene where we're dancing and I draw my hand slowly down her arm, she nearly drove me crazy—she literally couldn't shoot that scene without giggling all the way through, so we had to retake it about twenty-five times. Another moment I inserted was the line about listening to your heartbeat when you dance, and tapping Jennifer's hand on my chest. Moments like these added depth to the characters, and Jennifer came up with many of her own, too.

The more we added and revised, the stronger the characters got. But it wasn't just the rewrites that required us to put in serious overtime. We also spent hours perfecting the dance moves that would really make the movie pop. Lisa spent many late nights working with me, rehearsing and honing the dance scenes I'd shoot with Jennifer and Cynthia.

Following the lead of Kenny Ortega, who was like the Pied Piper, everyone in the cast spun and twirled and danced until we were ready to drop—Cynthia later said she lost ten pounds during the shoot, despite drinking milk shakes every day. But Kenny had an infectious energy. He was like Gene Kelly, whom he'd studied with. He was always dancing with a huge smile on his face, and having so much fun you couldn't help but have fun, too.

Kenny was a real hoofer, a talented dancer who could cross genre barriers. I loved the fact that he worked in so many kinds of dance—jazz, swing, salsa. Jazz in particular had been a very big part of my early dance education, since my mother had pretty much single-handedly created the jazz scene in Houston. So jazz dancing was in my soul, and I loved the feeling of loosening up my body, being able to use my shoulders and pelvis, allowing the sensuality to flow through with the music.

We all worked incredibly hard, but we had a hell of a lot of fun, too, especially during the scenes where the camp staff was dirty dancing after hours. Shooting those scenes really was like a party—just rock and roll and everybody sweating on the dance floor. The actors and dancers in the movie were so game and so talented, they just tore it up.

I drove the van between locations, with Kenny and Jennifer and Cynthia and whoever else wanted to come along. We all spent hours together in that van, singing songs and talking about the scenes. We were like a posse—a gang of young, energetic artists who'd been thrown together in this Podunk little town of Lake Lure, North Carolina, in a beautiful old colonial-style hotel, with nothing to do but create. It was one of the most exhausting shoots I can remember—but also one of the most fun.

•   •   •

With all the dancing and jumping and running around, it's no surprise that my knee began swelling again. I'd ice it after shooting the dance scenes, but as filming went on, I had to start getting it drained again—just as I'd done so often when dancing in New York. But it wasn't dancing that caused me the most knee pain of all. It was the scene where I'm balancing on the log with Jennifer.

We had to balance very carefully so we wouldn't tumble onto the rocks below. It looks like fun in the movie, but shooting that scene was dangerous and physically taxing. When you're balancing like that, your joints are working overtime, making constant tiny adjustments. And because most of the cartilage in my knee was gone, the bones were just grinding painfully on each other. After spending a couple of hours filming that log scene, I had to go straight to the hospital to get my knee drained. It was definitely more painful and difficult than anything I did on the dance floor.

In fact, I struggled constantly with Kenny and Emile to give me more serious dance moves. I wanted to show the audiences that although Johnny was blue-collar, he really could dance— throughout the shoot, I was dying to have Johnny show some real moves.

All the dirty dancing was fine, but I had to subordinate my ego for the role, as I was a more highly trained dancer than Johnny. In the end, the closest we got to letting Johnny do anything difficult was in the final scene of the movie, after I leaped off the stage. We spent hours rehearsing multiple different ways of doing the jump, and I leaped off that stage again and again, trying not to land too hard on my left knee because of the sheer number of times we shot it. But the real

dance move came after the jump, when I did a double pirou-
ette and double turn to the knee.

Shooting scenes indoors could also be unbearably hot, especially early on, when temperatures outside hit the nineties.
Inside, with the cameras and lights, temperatures soared to
above one hundred, and several dancers and actors passed out
from all the exertions. Paula Trueman, who played Mrs.
Schumacher, the wallet thief, even had to be taken to the hospital after fainting on the set. But with such a short shooting
schedule, everyone hung in there, fighting through the heat
to do multiple takes and get everything perfect.

Jennifer Grey worked as hard as anyone. And while she and
I had a rough start on *Red Dawn,* we ended up getting along
well during *Dirty Dancing.* But we did have a few moments of
friction when we were tired or after a long day of shooting.

I tend to be extremely focused when I'm working, and I like
to get down to business on the set. Jennifer was working her
ass off, and doing an amazing job considering the fact that she
had never been a professional dancer. But she also seemed
particularly emotional, sometimes bursting into tears if someone criticized her. And other times, she slipped into silly
moods, forcing us to do scenes over again when she'd start
laughing. I was on overdrive for the whole shoot—staying up
all night to do rewrites, squeezing in dance rehearsals, shooting various scenes—and was exhausted a lot of the time. So I
didn't have a whole lot of patience for doing multiple retakes.

The lift scene in the lake was a perfect example of how simultaneously fun and exhausting the shoot was. It was horrify-
ingly, hypothermically cold in that lake, and we filmed that
scene over and over. The crew had to build a platform under
the water—it would have been too deep otherwise—but when-

ever I slipped off that platform, I'd be treading water and scraping the shit out of my legs trying to get back on it quickly. And despite the fact that Jennifer was very light, when you're lifting someone in water, take after take after take, even the skinniest little girl can feel like five hundred pounds. By the time we finished shooting that sequence, my arms were like rubber, my body temperature had plunged, and my legs were a scraped-up mess.

But with that said, it was still a great feeling to lift Jennifer up in the middle of that beautiful setting, knowing the scene was going to look amazing. And despite any little irritations I felt, I have to say that overall, Jennifer did a truly phenomenal job.

In my life, I've encountered very few people who have the natural talent Jennifer has. She learned incredibly quickly, and she was game for anything. And as time went on, everything became easier for us both, because she never hit a plateau in terms of her ability or willingness to try new things. She had courage—emotional and physical courage—and the movie wouldn't have been half as good with anyone else in her role. I believe, and have for a long time, that Jennifer's performance was really underappreciated. In many ways, she made the movie.

As the summer turned to fall, we wrapped up filming. The shoot took only forty-four days, but because there had been a few delays, we ended up shooting later in the year than planned. The leaves had begun to turn at Lake Lure, so the crew rushed to spray-paint them back from orange and red into summer green for the last few scenes. Everyone—Emile, Kenny, Eleanor, and all the actors and dancers—seemed proud of what we'd done. And I felt really invested in this film, with all the dancing, acting, and rewriting. Not to mention the addition to the soundtrack of a song I wrote with Stacy Widelitz, "She's Like the Wind."

I've always written music, and I'd been singing onstage since my music theater days in Houston. I studied violin and guitar growing up, and ever since, there's nothing that relaxes me more than noodling around on a guitar and coming up with new melodies. While Lisa and I lived in New York, I played at a few Greenwich Village bars, trying out my own material and doing a few covers. Music has always been a huge part of my life, so it was natural to try to integrate it into my movies, too.

Stacy and I didn't write "She's Like the Wind" for *Dirty Dancing*—in fact, I started writing it for *Grandview, U.S.A.*, and Stacy later helped me finish it. I was disappointed when the song didn't make it into that film, but I didn't give up on it. While at Lake Lure, I played the demo for Emile, who liked it enough to pass it on to the music supervisor, Jimmy Ienner. Jimmy loved it, and he ended up picking it for an extended sequence in the film.

In the mid-1980s, movie soundtracks weren't a big business yet, so I wasn't thinking in terms of record sales at all—I was just happy that the song would finally get heard. Movie soundtracks had never been great sellers, so the music companies didn't charge much for the use of old songs. In fact, the entire *Dirty Dancing* soundtrack cost just two hundred thousand dollars. But this modest little soundtrack ended up changing the music business forever—just as this modest little $5.2 million movie would change all our lives forever. We just didn't know it yet.

•  •  •

After Emile and his team completed their final cut of *Dirty Dancing*, the producers set up a private screening so we could go see it before it was released. We'd heard that the first cut hadn't been very well received—in fact, one producer was rumored to have said, "Burn the negative and collect the insurance." But Emile had gone back into the editing room, determined to make the movie as great as we all envisioned it as being.

So, Lisa and I walked into that private screening knowing that everyone involved had done good work, but not having any idea what to expect beyond that. With all the thousands of little decisions that go into making a film—in writing, shooting, sound, lighting, cutting, editing—it's almost impossible to know how the final product will turn out.

We settled into our seats and the lights dimmed. Almost two hours later, when the credits rolled, Lisa and I turned to each other and smiled. The story had turned out better than we'd hoped for, all those months before in our kitchen. I thought it was a great teaching ground for mothers and young girls, a way to get into conversations about the birds and the bees. But what made me happiest was that it wasn't just a shallow movie about two people sucking face—it was a moment in time when these two very different souls really do connect. And Jennifer and I had achieved that together onscreen.

With all that said, we still figured it would be a modestly successful movie, and not much more than that. Lisa thought it was the kind of story people would be drawn to, where the good guy falls in love with the funky girl. We had no idea what

was coming—that after the movie opened we would be swallowed by a tidal wave of fame and attention, like nothing we'd
ever imagined.

In the meantime, Lisa and I headed for a place about as far
away from Hollywood as you can get—geographically, spiritually, and otherwise. We flew to Africa to make our first feature
together: *Steel Dawn*.

# Chapter 10

L isa and I peered out the window as the small plane we were in descended toward Swakopmund, on the western coast of Namibia. We were exhausted, having traveled for more than twenty-four hours, including a ten-hour layover in Frankfurt with nothing but chairs to sleep in. As we looked out at the desert terrain below, I said to Lisa, "Damn, it looks just like Arizona. Why'd we come all this way?"

Bone-tired from the *Dirty Dancing* shoot, I was only half joking. But we found out soon enough that the Namib Desert, where we would be shooting *Steel Dawn,* was a mystical and magical place. Our time spent doing this shoot would restore us in many ways, and lead to a lifelong love of Africa for both Lisa and me.

On our first day there, we piled into a Kombi Volkswagen van and headed out to explore. The Namib Desert borders the Kalahari, the second-largest desert in Africa after the Sahara. And although the word "desert" conjures images of sand and more sand, this desert was alive, especially in the morning.

In addition to beautifully wind-sculpted dunes, in some parts of the desert there were whole stretches of crusted black rock, like a moonscape. If you spend the night in that moon-scape, then wake up just before dawn, you can watch as the whole desert suddenly blossoms into green. When Lisa and I first saw it happen, we thought we were dreaming. But in actu-ality it was the lichen on the rocks opening up briefly, like a flower, to collect moisture. Then, as the sun rises in the sky, it suddenly closes back up, leaving nothing but scorched-looking rocks and the memory of what seemed like a mirage.

Ever since the days of camping with my dad in the back-woods of Texas, I've always loved learning about how people in different places live off the land. It's partly why *Red Dawn* appealed so much to me—I take a certain pride in knowing I could find a way to survive in any environment. Here in south-ern Africa, I wanted to connect with local people who could teach me how to live in the desert. Where do you find water, food, and shelter in such a desolate environment?

Seeing the desert blossom into green was amazing, and it showed us that sustenance can come from the most unlikely places. Some African members of the crew had grown up in the desert, and they told us more—about the roaming herds of ostrich and other animals, and details about how to survive in the desert. Both Lisa and I connected in a very deep way with the nature all around us, and we loved driving out to ex-plore different parts of the Kalahari during the shoot.

But although we loved being in Africa, I was exhausted from *Dirty Dancing*. I'd put everything I had into that shoot, and then we moved straight into *Steel Dawn* with no break. My *Steel Dawn* character, Nomad, is a warrior in a postapocalyptic world who travels across the desert fighting mutant sand peo-ple and outlaws. We shot a lot of very physical scenes, with sword fighting, martial arts, spear throwing, and hand-to-hand combat. All that activity, plus being immersed in this amazing place, was enough to make my head spin.

As always, Lisa was my rock. This was the first time we were acting in a movie together, and it was rewarding to share scenes with her onscreen, rather than just working behind the scenes with her. She played Kasha, a widow who lives in the desert with her young son and falls in love with Nomad. Lisa is a wonderful actress, and I was happy she was finally getting an opportunity to show her stuff. And I found that I was falling in love with her all over again, which led to a funny encounter with a woman who was working on the crew.

We were at a big cast-and-crew party toward the end of the shoot. Lisa and I danced together most of the night, and often had our arms around each other, which we'd been doing a lot of during our weeks in Africa. But at this party, one woman who worked in the wardrobe department kept giving Lisa the evil eye. She'd see us and just shake her head, or stand glaring at Lisa with a big frown on her face.

As it turned out, the woman knew I was married, but she didn't realize Lisa was my wife! She thought we were having a "set romance"—which, believe me, happens on movie sets just as often as you might imagine. But finally, someone told her Lisa and I were married, and she sheepishly came up and apologized to Lisa, who just laughed it off. Lisa had already dealt with a few women on other sets who disliked her *because* she was married to me, so this probably felt like a relief.

I'd always said that the perfect woman for me is someone who's interested in all the things I like to do—not someone who says, "No, I don't want to get my hair wet!" When we were shooting *Steel Dawn,* I saw once again how open Lisa was to new experiences. She loved going out into the desert, and loved learning everything about Africa. Spiritually and emotionally, we're just amazingly compatible.

After we wrapped *Steel Dawn*, we went on a safari, staying at the same place—Mala Mala—where Elizabeth Taylor and Richard Burton were married. It was incredibly romantic, a beautiful bungalow situated in the lush African landscape. By the end of our time in Africa, we felt refreshed and renewed. And it was a good thing, too—because when we got back to the United States and *Dirty Dancing* exploded into theaters, our relationship would be tested like never before.

The Deauville American Film Festival takes place every year in a beautiful resort town on France's Normandy coast. It's a prestigious festival, attended by the biggest movie stars, directors, and producers in the world. And in 1987, to our excitement, the organizers chose *Dirty Dancing* to open the festival.

Emile and Eleanor both flew to Deauville for the screening, and Lisa and I joined them there. We weren't sure what kind of reception the movie would get, since the French are very discerning moviegoers, and this was just a modest little film about 1960s America. We settled into our balcony seats and waited nervously as the lights dimmed. And as we watched *Dirty Dancing* all the way through for just the second time, I was struck again by how well it had turned out. But we still weren't sure what the audience was thinking.

When the movie ended and the lights came on, we stood up to leave. But all of a sudden, everyone in the theater turned around, looked up at us in the balcony, and broke into a thundering standing ovation that must have gone on for five minutes. Emile, Eleanor, Lisa, and I just stood there, dumbstruck, as the audience whooped and applauded. It was an incredibly gratifying moment, and gave us our first hint about how this "little movie" would ultimately be received.

A party had been planned for after the screening, and it seemed as if half of Deauville showed up. After a sit-down dinner, the music came on, and everyone danced into the wee hours of the morning, trying out their dirty-dancing moves and bringing a little bit of Lake Lure to the French coast. It was the perfect kickoff to a crazy time.

*Dirty Dancing* opened in the United States on August 21, 1987. It shot to the number-two spot, and within ten days it had sold more than $10 million in tickets—a huge amount back then. People went to see it multiple times, starting a trend that would ultimately shoot the grosses to more than $60 million in 1987 alone. *Dirty Dancing*, made for just over $5 million, was on its way to becoming a bona fide phenomenon.

If *North and South* had made me a household name, *Dirty Dancing* blew the lid off. It was everywhere you looked—on TV, in magazines and newspapers, and playing on multiple screens at the cineplexes. People dissected Johnny and Baby's relationship, debated about Penny's abortion, and talked about their own relationships with their fathers. We had never dreamed the movie would become anywhere near this big. But suddenly we were engulfed in a total whirlwind.

Lisa and I had gotten used to people stopping us on the street and asking for autographs, but now everything got turned up a few more notches. Rather than having a couple of people approach us politely, we were getting mobbed. People were knocking on the windows of our car, surrounding us as we walked into restaurants. Paparazzi began trailing us and even hanging around outside Rancho Bizarro, waiting for us to come out. We were thrilled at the success of *Dirty Dancing*, but on the other hand, it was becoming harder and harder to live anything like a normal life outside the haven of our ranch.

It's hard to describe exactly what it feels like to be thrust into this kind of fame, but "whirlwind" comes pretty close. Everything around you is just spinning. You try to touch it, to get a grasp on it, but it just spins faster and faster. If I had found myself in the middle of something like this when I was younger, when I first came to Hollywood, it probably would have destroyed me. In many ways, dealing with fame is the purest form of dealing with your demons.

The easiest way to destroy people is to give them exactly what they want. You might not realize it at the time, but the struggle to achieve something is, in many ways, much more satisfying than actually getting it. The very act of striving is what keeps you alive, and it keeps you grounded. But then, when the thing you've been fighting for is suddenly in your grasp, it's all too easy to look around and say—is that all there is?

Also, despite how proud I was of finally making it big, I was also torn about how I'd finally gotten to this place. All the fears I had about giving in to "dancer-turned-actor" typecasting were crystallized one evening when Lisa and I happened to catch a segment about *Dirty Dancing* on *Entertainment Tonight*.

We were getting ready to go out of town, and had the TV on in the background as we were packing. I heard the announcer say something like, "After the break, Patrick Swayze bumps and grinds his way into movie history!" My heart sank. I turned and looked at Lisa, who just shook her head. This was it—my worst nightmare come to life. I'd worked so hard to be taken seriously, and now this would be my legacy. I was definitely proud of the movie, but "bumping and grinding" was not what I wanted to be remembered for.

Yet it wasn't only my role as Johnny Castle that was stirring up the whirlwind. The *Dirty Dancing* soundtrack, made for just two hundred thousand dollars, also shot to number one on the Billboard charts—and it stayed there for eighteen weeks. "She's Like the Wind," the single I wrote with Stacy Widelitz and performed with Wendy Fraser, went to number three on the Billboard Hot 100 chart and number one on Contemporary Adult. Along with "I've Had the Time of My Life," it became one of the signature songs of *Dirty Dancing*.

Lisa and I flew to New York City for a record signing at the height of the *Dirty Dancing* craze. I was scheduled to sign copies from nine or ten o'clock in the morning, but when the reps picked us up in a limo and brought us to the Sam Goody store, we could see that people were already lined up all the way around the block and beyond. "They've been lining up since about 6:00 A.M.," one guy told us, "just sitting out there on the sidewalk."

The limo pulled up outside the store, and about fifteen security guys materialized to shepherd us through the crowds. Everyone started screaming when Lisa and I got out of the car—it was a madhouse. We had to go only twenty feet or so, from the curb to the door, but hundreds of women were pressing in, trying to get a glimpse of us. The noise was deafening, and the whole experience was absolutely surreal.

When we made it into the store, we could see all the fans outside, lined up and pressing against the huge plate-glass windows. It was a vast sea of humanity, waiting for a few seconds of conversation, maybe a snapshot, and an autograph. My head was spinning, taking everything in, when the guy from the store leaned down and said to me, "Now you know what it's like to be the Beatles." And he was right. Looking out those windows was just like looking at those vintage reels of screaming fans.

But strangely enough, when you're in a sea of people like that, it's actually a very lonely feeling. I was glad to have Lisa at my side, glad not to be facing this pandemonium alone. She stayed nearby as I smiled until my face hurt and signed so many CDs that my hand began to cramp. I kept going well past the allotted time, because I couldn't imagine turning someone away who'd waited for hours on the sidewalk, and who was looking for only a few seconds of my time. So we stayed and stayed, until the last person had gotten through the line.

And it was like that every time people wanted autographs. If one person stopped me on the sidewalk to sign something, and someone else came up, then another, I'd end up standing there until everyone had come and gone. Once, at a baseball game, I must have signed a thousand autographs. These people were paying me the ultimate compliment, and the last thing I wanted was for anyone to walk away thinking I had too big a head to find a moment for them. It was my Texas manners coming through, but also my desire to be liked.

This could be hard on Lisa, though, especially if we needed to get somewhere, or we were hungry, or just needed to go to the bathroom. Once I even made her stand in the snow, shivering in the cold in high heels and a little dress. Learning how to balance the needs of the fans with Lisa's needs, and my own, was a process that took some time.

The one thing I couldn't abide was when people got aggressive. I'll spend all day accommodating you if you're polite about it, but if you're rude, that's another story. But even so,

In *Red Dawn*, I got to ride horses, shoot bazookas, and fight the Communists in the ruggedly beautiful mountains of New Mexico. It was a grueling shoot, but I loved every minute of it.

On Fancy, the horse I rode in *Red Dawn*. We took him back to LA with us after the shoot. ("RED DAWN" © Metro-Goldwyn-Mayer Studios Inc. All Rights Reserved. Courtesy of MGM Clip + Still)

Lisa, Nicholas Gunn, and I wrote and performed *Without a Word*, a cathartic play about dance. Our cast and crew gave their hearts and souls. Left to right: MB Gordy, Nicholas, Griff Griffis, Lisa, Stacy Widelitz, Mark Paskell, me, Michael Wise (not pictured: Jack Magee).

Playing Orry Main in *North and South* sent my career
soaring. I loved playing the courageous southern gentleman—
give me a cape, a sword, and a horse, and I'm a happy man.
(© American Broadcasting Companies, Inc.)

Jennifer Grey and I pose at the Academy Awards. *Dirty Dancing* was supposed to be a sweet little movie, but it surprised everyone by becoming a blockbuster. (Photo: Jim Smeal/WireImage/Getty Images)

Lifting Jennifer in the lake looked fun. But the freezing water and multiple takes on the small slippery platform I was standing on made it very difficult. (Still taken from "DIRTY DANCING" provided through the courtesy of Lion's Gate)

It was an amazing experience to dance down that aisle in a style that was created just for this movie. (Still taken from "DIRTY DANCING" provided through the courtesy of Lion's Gate)

Lisa joined me at a signing of the *Dirty Dancing* sound track at a Sam Goody store in New York City. Unbelievably, thousands had lined up on the sidewalk since early that morning. Fun to be a rock star for a day. (Trans World Entertainment Corporation d/b/a f.y.e. for your entertainment and Sam Goody in addition to websites fye.com and samgoody.com)

On the set of *Steel Dawn*, the first movie Lisa and I starred in together.
We explored the Kalahari Desert and fell in love with Africa
during this shoot.

With Liam Neeson and Bill Paxton on the set of *Next of Kin*. I've gotten to work with
some great people over the years.

Rehearsing for *Road House* with kickboxing champion Benny "The Jet" Urquidez, who helped me find my fighting style by training to the sounds of Michael Jackson's "Thriller." (Photo by Peter Sorel)

Lisa and I got seriously into showing Arabian horses—the steeds of the gods. Here, we pose with our champion Arabian stallion Tammen, a magnificent, beautiful animal. (Photo by Javan Schaller)

Whoopi Goldberg was perfect for the role of Oda Mae Brown in *Ghost*. It didn't matter what was in the script—she just said whatever the hell popped into her head. And it was hilarious. (Photo by Peter Sorel)

Warning: Don't try this at home. Making a plaster-cast dummy for Sam Wheat's death scene in *Ghost* made me claustrophobic for years.

Three of the great ladies I've had the good fortune to work with. Melanie Griffith (*Forever Lulu*), Demi Moore, and Whoopi Goldberg. (Photo: Albert Ferreira/startraksphoto.com. Courtesy of Planet Hollywood)

Patsy Swayze, my proud mama, named me "Patrick Swayze" because she thought it would look good on a marquee. (Photo by Michael Montfort)

Hollywood isn't just about acting, it's also about the dog-and-pony show of appearances, interviews, and photo shoots. *Ghost* intensified the whirlwind. (Photo: SGranitz/ WireImage/Getty Images)

Lisa and I pose with our Rhodesian Ridgeback Jazz, in front of our beloved Cessna 414 Chancellor. We both got our pilot's licenses and love to fly.

Swayze with an attitude. (Photo by Peggy Sirota)

With director Roland Joffé on the set of *City of Joy* in Calcutta. India was a land of intense squalor and generosity of spirit, and the shoot was life-changing. (Photo by David Appleby)

My imitation of Miss Kitty on *Gunsmoke*. With John Leguizamo and Wesley Snipes on the set of *To Wong Foo, Thanks for Everything, Julie Newmar*. (Getty Images Entertainment)

'rust is everything in relationships with animals. Here, I'm throwing Cody, our beloved Rhodesian Ridgeback, into the air while our Standard Poodle, Derek, watches. (Photo by Bruce Weber)

It's a bird! It's a plane! It's me just starting my skydiving training for *Point Break* with Jim Wallace.

I was lucky to survive my off-airport landing in June 2000. It's a scary thing to have landed a plane and not remember how you did it.
(Getty Images Entertainment)

Lisa, George de la Peña, and I dance in *One Last Dance*, the movie we made based on *Without a Word*. This marked a turning point for Lisa, who directed, wrote, produced, and starred in the film. (WAW Productions LLC)

For my 2009 TV series *The Beast*, I shot thirteen episodes in Chicago while undergoing chemotherapy. Lisa directed my favorite one, "Brother's Keeper." (Photo by Amy Holliday Sobin)

At home with Lisa and our dogs—two of whom seem to be
enjoying themselves a little too much.
(Photo by Joan Lauren)

when people did get rude, I was still never comfortable just walking away. I wanted to find a way to turn the energy positive again.

Once, I was scheduled to make an appearance onstage in West Germany, and even though there were at least a dozen bodyguards, the crowd managed to break through. Suddenly, people were climbing over people and grabbing at me, and the bodyguards were completely overwhelmed. They started pushing back at the fans, which threatened to make a bad situation worse—and the last thing we needed was for a riot to break out.

Suddenly, I had an idea. Rather than resisting the crowd or trying to push back, I just started shaking hands. "Nice to meet you!" I'd say, shaking a hand, then following with, "No need to push. How you doing? I'm Patrick. Let's make some room here." I shouted to the bodyguards to do the same. "Say hello to people! Shake a hand, keep smiling." When the bodyguards started doing the same, turning the energy from hostile to friendly, the fans soon stopped shoving.

I learned little techniques like that for crowd control, like patting someone on the back as you shake hands, then gently guiding them to one side. The fact is, once you've talked with people and given them that moment they were looking for, they're on your side. So you can easily turn a group of fans into a second line of defense if others are pushing and shoving. The most important thing to remember is that the people who are pushing at you really want only one thing: for you to look into their eyes and say, "Hey, how are you doing? Nice to meet you." And I was always happy to do that.

The first time Lisa and I really saw what it meant to be famous was back in my *Skatetown, U.S.A.* days. Jaclyn Smith, whom we knew from Houston, had become a huge star in *Charlie's Angels,* and she came to the *Skatetown* premiere as a show of support. Lisa and I watched in amazement as she walked out of the premiere and flashbulbs began popping like strobe lights. I was feeling blinded by all those flashes, but Jackie had the most beautiful smile on her face, and she barely blinked. She knew she had to look good, so she had a completely calm expression, as if she was the only one there. I often thought of her example all those years later, when I became the one in the strobe lights.

Unfortunately, there's a flip side to all the love you get from fans. The vast majority are perfectly decent people who reach out with an open heart. But once you become famous, some others crawl out of the woodwork—the ones who don't hesitate to go after your money and your reputation, hoping to enrich themselves.

People will sue you for any little thing, claiming you bumped into their car with yours, or even that you injured them somehow with an innocuous handshake. And every incident requires a response from a lawyer. We've had a wonderful lawyer for years, Fred Gaines, who takes care of any issue that comes up, but the fact is, having to respond to every claim takes money and time, even if the claim is totally fabricated.

After "She's Like the Wind" became a hit, at least five people filed lawsuits claiming they'd written it. Never mind the fact that if all five of these people truly believed they'd written it, they probably ought to be suing each other, too. These claims just came out of nowhere, from people we'd never met, and one suit even went so far that Stacy and I were no longer allowed to receive royalties. It just dragged on and on, but I knew we'd win because we had written the song. So Fred just kept responding, point by point, and we figured the truth would eventually come out.

And it did, when the plaintiffs submitted their account of when they'd written the song. They claimed they wrote it just before *Dirty Dancing* began shooting—but of course, Stacy and I had written it, and even recorded a master, during *Grandview, U.S.A.* back in 1984. I dug up that master and sent it to Fred, and that finally ended the lawsuit. But because it had dragged on so long to begin with, whoever sued us certainly felt the pain in their own wallets—just as they should have.

After supposedly "bumping and grinding" my way into movie history, I signed on next to do a serious family drama called *Tiger Warsaw.* I played a drug- and alcohol-addicted loner whose sister accuses him of committing incest—a dark, intense movie that pushed me deeper as an actor but ultimately never really came together. Despite having a strong cast, including the Oscar-nominated actress Piper Laurie, *Tiger Warsaw* was directed by Amin Q. Chaudhri, an inexperienced director who made some questionable choices. The film didn't do well, making little more than a ripple at the box office.

But the film I shot after that, *Road House,* did very big business at the box office. And while *Dirty Dancing* had launched a kind of cult following for me among women, *Road House* created a cult following of its own among men. With its multiple bar-fight scenes and macho, tough-shit antagonists, it was a classic guys' film.

The truth is, in some ways I was built to be an action star. All the running, jumping, and falling I did as a kid had taught me how to be my own stuntman. Gymnastics had strengthened every part of my body and taught me balance. Studying martial arts, boxing, and sword fighting gave me a base of skills I could use in any kind of fight scene. And I could race anything—cars, motorcycles, horses, whatever was called for.

*Road House* was an old-fashioned Western-style movie, where the good guy comes to a bad town to clean it up. I knew it wasn't Dostoevsky, but I still wanted to give my character, Dalton, real depth, and not just play him as a campy hero. There's definitely a guilty pleasure to watching and loving *Road House,* but it ended up entertaining a lot of people, especially men who liked watching a stand-up guy like Dalton, who had a strong code.

For the fight scenes in *Road House,* I trained with Benny "the Jet" Urquidez, a kickboxing pro who never lost a professional match. Benny was a short, stocky guy who used sharp, sudden moves to keep his opponents off balance. But when he tried to teach his style to me, I had a lot of trouble—it's just not the way I move. I kept trying to mimic his technique, but we weren't getting anywhere.

Suddenly, Benny said, "Wait a minute! You're a dancer! I've got an idea." The next day, he showed up on set with a boom box. He plugged it in and flipped a switch, and Michael Jackson's "Thriller" came blasting out.

That was all it took. Moving with the beat of Michael Jackson's music, I finally got a rhythm going, and my kickboxing came together. It was a great moment—all the syncopation, speed, and subtlety of the art form suddenly were mine. And I loved it. I hadn't done any martial arts for a while, but after studying with Benny, I got right back into it. *Road House* gave me the opportunity to hone an old skill that I never realized I'd missed.

I soon found out that I'd need all the fighting skills I could muster for this movie. Because the actor who played my primary opponent, Marshall Teague, was ready to kick my ass for real if he could get away with it.

From the very beginning, Marshall, who played the bad-guy enforcer Jimmy, treated me like some snot-nose know-nothing actor. He had served in Vietnam and was a Navy SEAL—which meant he was a serious, real-life badass. He had no patience for bullshit and would say so to anyone's face. Marshall apparently thought I was a dilettante pretty boy he could knock over with one of his meaty fingers. But when we started training, he learned otherwise.

He and I started rehearsing our fight scenes, and soon enough he saw that I knew what I was doing, and that I could take a punch. "Let's put some contact into it," I told him, well aware that he could lay me flat out if he chose to. But I knew if we choreographed it well, we could have some contact without killing each other, and it would look amazingly real onscreen.

When you earn the respect of a man like Marshall, you earn it for life. He and I became friends on the set of *Road House,* and we've been friends ever since. Not that many people understood his mentality, but when I looked him in the eye, we really connected. It was a good thing, too, because the fight scene we shot was absolutely epic, and we very nearly killed each other.

We fought in a river, and I was wearing nothing but little hip-hugger sweatpants—no shirt, no pads, no nothing. So when I hit the ground, I was hitting the ground hard. Since both Marshall and I loved the adrenaline high of a fight, it was easy to get carried away, and we really started pounding on each other in this scene.

After a few minutes of us punching and kicking the shit out of each other, Marshall picked up a log and swung it over his head. My eyes got wide as I realized he was about to break it right over my back. Marshall apparently thought it was a prop log, which would have been perfect for the scene—but unfortunately, it wasn't. He realized his mistake midswing, but it was too late: He cracked me right across the spine with a real log, breaking a couple of my ribs and knocking the wind out of me.

I dropped to my hands and knees, gasping for breath, but the scene called for us to keep fighting. I didn't break character and didn't give up—we kept fighting, and eventually got to the part where Dalton is forced to kill Jimmy. When you watch this scene in the movie, the exhaustion you see on my face is absolutely real. I barely had the strength to drag myself out of the river after that fight.

My next role was as another tough guy, a Chicago cop named Truman Gates in *Next of Kin*. But this time, the training I got wasn't nearly as enjoyable as studying kickboxing with Benny the Jet. This time, some real Chicago cops decided they'd give me some training I would never forget.

They hung out with me on the set, took me on ride-alongs to get a feel for the streets, and told me all about the dangers they faced on the job. We spent a lot of time together, and I really bonded with these guys. They were the real deal, putting their lives on the line every day, and I respected their courage. Then they decided to test mine. Or at least, test how strong my stomach was.

They drove me to the Chicago morgue, pulling the squad car up out front. I already knew what I was in for—they were going to show me dead and decomposing bodies, to test my mettle. But before that happened, there was a funny moment out on the sidewalk.

The cops were walking me up to the door, when a couple of junkies lying out front, really desperate-looking guys, peered up at me. Through a heroin-induced haze, one of them squinted and said, "Hey! Aren't you that Dirty Dance dude?" I couldn't believe it—these guys couldn't have been to a movie in years, but I guess *Dirty Dancing* was everywhere you looked at that point, in newspapers, magazines, on posters, all over the place. But I just smiled and said, "Nope, sorry. You've got the wrong guy." And the cops hustled me through the door.

It was a beautiful building, all pristine and pretty on the outside and nice and clean on the inside. But then the guys led me down into the bowels of the place, where the bodies were stored.

The first thing that amazed me was how many bodies there were. The ceilings were about fifty feet up, and there were rows and rows of shelves with nothing but body parts on them—a head, an arm, a hand, a torso, a leg. Some of them had apparently been there a long time, as they were in a pretty advanced state of decomposition.

The guys chose a particularly gruesome body to show me first, hoping to make me puke. It was a kind of tough-guy game—could I stand to see and smell all this, or was my stomach too weak? These guys had seen everything already, so they had a clinical detachment. They just wanted to see whether I could handle it. I couldn't, but I didn't let on. I felt the bile rise in my throat and started to throw up, but managed to swallow it back down. It sounds disgusting, and it was, but I wasn't about to show these cops that I couldn't handle it.

There was another, more serious reason I didn't want to show weakness. Doing this kind of training for a movie is all about showing someone else's world on film. The story is really about them, and what they do, and they're teaching you out of pride. I wanted to be good for these guys. In fact, I wanted to *be* these guys on film. It was the least I could do for them. So I forced myself to behave and respond as they would. And just as I respected them, they respected my efforts to make my portrayal of their world absolutely true and real.

Lisa was also up for a role in *Next of Kin,* playing Truman Gates's wife, Jessie. Once again, she would have been perfect for it—but she was reluctant to appear to be pushing for it as my real-life wife. Lisa has a lot of integrity, and it really came through in instances like these, where she didn't push as hard for roles she could have won. Helen Hunt, who'd just started her career, ended up getting the role—and she was wonderful. But it was frustrating for Lisa, who's a very talented actress.

The truth is, talent takes you only so far in Hollywood. There are any number of other factors that influence who makes it—and Lisa was up against some real obstacles from the get-go. For one thing, people in Hollywood have a thing about husbands and wives. The William Morris Agency, one of the most powerful in the industry, won't represent husband-wife teams. There's a perception of nepotism, even where there isn't any.

A lot of people didn't take Lisa as seriously as they should have, just because she was married to me. If I pushed for her to get a role, that was seen as favoritism—even if she was the best actress for it. She had to work twice as hard and be twice as good to be taken half as seriously, which is very hard to overcome.

Another big issue was that you really have to be able to sell yourself in Hollywood. As a Texan, that was something I loved to do—I loved the challenge of winning someone over, making that person want to hire me. Being from a Finnish family, Lisa had inherited a certain reserve. She had been raised to believe that the quality of what you do should speak for itself, and that if you try to sell to people, you're insulting their intelligence. If success in Hollywood came from sheer talent, Lisa would have been a huge star. But all these factors conspired to keep her down—which was a real source of frustration for her.

Lisa kept pushing and working, though, and she got a recurring role in the TV series *Max Headroom*, playing a character named Janie Crane. She went out for auditions whenever we were in Los Angeles, but much of the time she was working with me on my movie sets—rewriting and helping me with my scenes and performance. Every movie I've ever been in, Lisa has had a significant role in fleshing out my character. She also started learning the tools of the director's trade, spending time with the director of photography on each set and asking about the how and the why of a shot, becoming savvy about the inner workings and process of making a movie. Some spouses came to movie sets to relax, but Lisa always came to work and learn.

Liam Neeson and Bill Paxton were both in *Next of Kin*, and we became great friends. Liam and I enjoyed hitting the town together, a couple of Irish guys going to Chicago's blues clubs and pounding the beers. He was a wild man with a sweet, gentle side, and as my dad used to say, he could charm the rassling suit off a pissant. Years later, when his wife, Natasha Richardson, died at age forty-five after a freak skiing accident, I felt for him like a brother.

With *Next of Kin* and *Road House,* I'd now done two macho action flicks in a row. I didn't mind showcasing that side of myself, and of course I'd had a blast making those movies. I also had original songs in both those movies, so even though I was playing the action star, I still got to show some versatility behind the scenes. But I was feeling the itch again to get a deeper, more fleshed-out role, so I could stretch myself more as an actor.

The next movie I auditioned for would give me exactly that—but I'd have to get past an extremely reluctant director if I ever hoped to get cast.

# Chapter 11

One afternoon in late 1988, Lisa walked up to me in the dining room and dropped a script on the table. "Buddy," she said, "you have to read this. It's incredible." I looked down at the title page and saw the word "Ghost."

After *Dirty Dancing* became a hit, I'd started receiving all kinds of scripts, which were soon piled up on bedside tables, chairs, and coffee tables all over the house. I even got offered money to read some of them, but there just weren't enough hours in the day to do everything that needed doing, and then have time to read scripts. So although I trusted Lisa's opinion more than anyone's, I left the script right where she'd put it.

It was still there a month later. Lisa saw it on the table and said, "Buddy, *please* read this! It's a great story, and you'll love the part!" I promised her I'd get to it, and I really did mean to, but it wasn't until Lisa enlisted our assistant Rosi to double-team me, nagging me in her English accent, "Patrick! Read the script!" that I finally sat down and looked at the first page.

And that was all it took—I didn't stop reading until I'd gotten all the way through. When I turned the final page, I walked into the kitchen with tears in my eyes. "I have to do this movie,"

I told Lisa. The story was every bit as good as she'd said it was, and she was right—the role of Sam Wheat was perfect for me.

Unfortunately, the director, Jerry Zucker, didn't think so. In fact, his response when my name came up for a possible audition was to say, "Patrick Swayze? Over my dead body!" Jerry had just seen the kickboxing, long-haired, tough-guy Patrick in *Road House,* and he just couldn't imagine me in the role of the sensitive boyfriend who gets murdered and comes back as a ghost.

Of course, Jerry himself knew a little bit about going against type. He'd made his name doing a string of off-the-wall comedies, from *Airplane* to *Top Secret* to *Ruthless People,* and *Ghost* would be his first real foray into drama. He obviously believed it was possible to move successfully between genres. Now I just had to convince him I could do it as well as he could.

Demi Moore had already been cast as Molly Jensen, beating out several other actresses who auditioned, including Nicole Kidman, Molly Ringwald, and Meg Ryan. And a Who's Who of leading men were under consideration for the part of Sam, including Kevin Bacon, Alec Baldwin, Tom Cruise, Harrison Ford, and Tom Hanks, but the role was still open. Zucker was absolutely convinced I was the wrong guy for the role, but he finally agreed to at least let me audition for it.

Sam Wheat is a banker, and I wanted to really look the part, so I dressed in a sharp Kenzo suit and tied my hair—still long from *Next of Kin*—back into a ponytail. I walked into the audition, faced Jerry Zucker and casting director Jane Jenkins, and said, "Do whatever you need to do to check me out. I'm willing to do this entire script from beginning to end if you want."

And they almost did. They really put me through my paces, asking me to do six scenes. Jane read the part of Molly, and I put everything I had into the scenes. I wanted this part so badly I could taste it. Jane could feel it, too—as she told Lisa later, she had tears in her eyes at a couple of points. She said it felt so real, and so emotional, it made her miss being an actress. It was an intense audition, and when it was over Jerry Zucker was completely convinced. I'd won the part of Sam.

That left one more role to cast: Oda Mae Brown. When I first read the script, I immediately thought of Whoopi Goldberg for the part of the spirit medium, but Jerry didn't want to consider her. Whoopi's career had begun to take off in the eighties, starting with her one-woman show on Broadway, *The Spook Show,* and soaring higher with her starring role as Celie in *The Color Purple.* She was an amazingly gifted comic, but she also had incredible range as an actress. She was perfect, but Jerry thought of her mostly as a comic, and he feared her comedic edge would overshadow the relationship between Molly and Sam, which he saw as the heart of the story.

In the meantime, Jerry and Jane sent out feelers to numerous other actresses. Tina Turner, Oprah Winfrey, Patti Labelle, and others got the call, but none of them worked out. I kept telling Jerry that Whoopi was perfect, but he just wouldn't hear of it. Finally, I insisted. "Jerry, at least just put me in a room together with her," I said. "We'll see if there's any chemistry."

At the time, Whoopi was shooting *The Long Walk Home* in Alabama with Sissy Spacek. Whoopi knew she had been passed over for Oda Mae, and that dozens of other actresses had been considered. When she finally got the call, she told Jerry she couldn't leave the set to fly back to LA for an audition. We would need to come out to Alabama if we wanted her.

So both Jerry and I flew out to meet with Whoopi. She and

I had met once, briefly, after her Broadway show, but we didn't know each other. But as soon as we started going through Sam and Oda Mae's scenes, you could feel the electricity popping in the air. Whoopi just took those lines and created a fully fleshed, finger-wagging, hip-shaking character all her own.

Once again, Jerry admitted that his first instincts had been wrong. Whoopi was perfect. He offered her the role, and I couldn't wait for us all to get back to LA to start shooting. But first, as with all my movies, it was time to do some rewrites.


In the first draft of *Ghost* that Lisa and I read, the character of Sam couldn't communicate with the living after he died, so he just hovered around in scenes, with no more lines. Maybe that seems logical for a ghost, but both Lisa and I felt the scenes would play out a lot better if Sam continued to be an active character.

That's a pretty major change to suggest, but fortunately the writer, Bruce Joel Rubin, is not your ordinary writer. We forged an instant bond with him, and he was always open to whatever changes we suggested. Of all the writers I've worked with over the years, I felt the closest connection with Bruce—he really became like a brother to me. And as I learned later, he was the one who suggested early on that Jerry consider me for the role of Sam.

I knew that if Sam was relegated to being just a silent apparition in the corner, we'd miss out on all kinds of dramatic and humorous possibilities. "The humor comes from this guy who refuses to accept that he's dead," I said to Bruce. "He keeps trying to participate with the people who are alive. So let's make him part of the scenes, give him dialogue." Fortunately, Bruce agreed.

All three of the main characters needed some rewriting, and we worked on them throughout the first weeks of the shoot. But with Whoopi, it didn't really matter what was on the page—what came out of her mouth when the cameras were rolling was whatever the hell popped into her head.

This is Whoopi's genius: She just goes wherever her instinctual wild-ass world happens to take her. She has so much trust in herself, so much trust in her own instincts, that it freed me up, too. The one thing I knew about comedy was, you shouldn't play things for laughs. The best comedy is born out of reality. So when Whoopi was doing her free-form thing, I played Sam's natural reactions to her—and those funny moments were some of the best in the film.

This also played into an acting technique I'd been using for years. I like to look at every other relationship and every other character before I really look at mine. It keeps me out of my own ego when I approach my character, and also, you learn a lot about people by looking at how they relate to others. Playing Sam straight up, responding to Whoopi's comedy riffs, was the most honest and direct way to bring out his true character.

Demi and I did the same thing when we shot the pottery scene—we played off each other and really made up the scene as we went along. It was pretty sexy playing in all that clay, so all we had to do was go with it, let our imaginations run wild, and then touch each other's arms for the sparks to fly. The best love scenes don't require what I call "humpage"—in fact, that often takes away from the tension. You don't really want to see the characters jumping each other's bones. You want to

see them looking intently into each other's eyes, in an intimate, personal moment that conveys desire. That's what I feel
is sexy.

Shooting love scenes is really difficult. It's such a private
thing, and you're on a set with camera operators, director,
lighting technicians—sometimes a dozen or more people milling around. You're trying to make a moment look sexy, in just
about the most unsexy environment there is. And I always felt
extra pressure, since I was supposed to be Mr. Sexy, if you believed all the magazines. Of all the scenes I ever shot, I probably felt least confident about the love scenes. So it's ironic that
the clip of Demi and me at the pottery wheel is one of the best
known of my whole career.

You can't really choreograph or script love scenes. You just
have to have a conversation between the actors and the director, talk about what you want the viewers to feel—and then
dive right into it, nerves and all. Luckily for me, Demi was
really good in these situations. She was very warm—much
warmer than she'd been in the other scenes we shot together.
She showed a vulnerability that was very attractive, and that
really came through onscreen. When Lisa and I saw the finished film months later, I was happy—and relieved—with how
it turned out. Demi and I had managed to capture a moment
between these two people that made everything that happened later in the story feel that much more wrenching and
emotional.

And speaking of wrenching and emotional, there was one
scene that nearly tore me apart when we shot it. I didn't have
any idea it would be so devastating, but I could hardly even get
through it while the cameras rolled. The scene that broke my
heart was when Sam looks down on his own bloody body in

Molly's arms and realizes he's dead. A lot of people assume that scene was done with a camera trick—that the body lying on the ground is me, and that we shot the scene twice. But Demi was actually holding an incredibly realistic life-size dummy of me. In the scene, Sam sprints after the guy who's just killed him, then walks back slowly toward Molly, realizing as he draws near that he can see someone in her arms. As the cameras were rolling, I walked up to Demi holding the dummy, but when I looked down at the body a terrible chill shot right through me.

I suddenly flashed back to the moment when I was looking down at my father's body in his casket, eight years earlier—a moment I had completely blocked out. I don't look particularly like my dad, but somehow the dummy in Demi's arms just became him right then.

My whole body started shaking, and my heart pounded. I felt as if I was having a panic attack. I couldn't believe how strongly I felt my dad's presence in that moment. Jerry Zucker kept the cameras rolling, but he couldn't use this cut—it was too real, too intense, and audiences would have had a hard time switching back to the lighter feel of the movie. When Jerry finally yelled "Cut," I staggered away from Demi and tried to collect myself. We shot it again, and the second time I managed to play the scene. But I've never forgotten that sickening feeling of horror I felt.

And that wasn't even the first time I freaked out in connection with that scene. The first time came when we actually made the dummy. Jerry wanted it to look exactly like me, which meant I'd have to get a plaster likeness made. It's not a pleasant experience, believe me.

The special-effects department sent me to a makeup room,

where they asked me to take off my shirt and sit on a stool. The dummy needs to be made with the exact pose and expression required for the shot, which in this case meant I'd have to mimic lying dead on the street. We figured out the best facial expression and how I needed to hold my arms, and then a couple of guys got to work.

They started layering me with wet plaster strips from the waist up, creating the dummy's torso. Then, they created a jig system to prop my arms in place, since I'd have to hold them still until the plaster was applied and had dried. They kept laying those plaster strips on me, working their way up my body to my neck, then my chin, then my mouth. Then suddenly I realized, *Wait a minute! They're going to bury me in this shit!* At the last moment, they stuck a couple of straws into my nostrils so I could breathe—but already I could feel some of the liquid from the wet plaster seeping into my mouth and inching down my throat.

I felt as if I was about to suffocate. I'd never been claustrophobic in my life, but being completely encased in this plaster cast, I was seriously freaking out. I couldn't see, smell, or hear, I could barely breathe, and foul-tasting liquid was seeping into my esophagus.

As panic rose in my chest, I started clearing my throat loudly, hoping the guys would realize what was going on. Finally, one of the guys asked, "Are you okay, Patrick?" I groaned, and he must have realized what was going on, because he poked a tongue depressor through the plaster covering my mouth, to let me get a little air in. I calmed down enough to sit still while the plaster dried, but once I got that cast off I swore I'd never do anything like that again. Ever since then, I've had little moments of claustrophobia, when scuba diving or in an enclosed space. I flash right back to that feeling of being trapped.

*Ghost* was the most high-tech movie I'd ever done. It wasn't easy back in 1989, when CGI technology was so new, to shoot a realistic-looking ghost scene. But we used a new technique that made the ghost scenes look real, even though some of the effects do seem dated now.

First, the actors would do a run-through of the scene, getting an idea of where each character would be. In the scene where Willy, the Bronx bad guy, breaks into Molly's house, we walked through the whole sequence: Sam sees him come in, realizes who he is, and tries in vain to stop him from going through the house. Sam still doesn't understand that he can't touch living people, so he takes swings at Willy, but his fist goes right through him. And when Willy tries to go upstairs, to Molly's bedroom, Sam hurls himself at him, desperate to find a way to stop him. But Willy never knows he's there.

Once we'd walked through the scene, the crew taped little numbers on the floor, showing us exactly where we had to be at each point in the action. I had a specific spot for every tiny moment, and not only did I have to be right on that spot, but my timing had to be absolutely perfect, because Jerry was going to shoot the whole sequence with each actor separately, and then layer them together to make it look as if we were in the room at the same time.

This would have been just about impossible to pull off, but we had a computerized camera that ensured the timing was perfect. When we first shot the scene, the camera recorded its own position, angles, and length of shots. It could then re-create the shoot precisely again—but with a different actor going through the scene. Using this camera meant that whatever the actors did, it would look as if they were together while the scene was being shot, since the camera angles were identical. So the only thing we had to do was make sure we hit our marks exactly—otherwise it might look like Sam was swinging at air, rather than throwing his fist through Willy's jaw.

Of course, hitting those marks so precisely is easier said than done. For the sequence where Sam chases Willy up and down the stairs, I was throwing myself all over the place, diving, falling, rolling. It's hard enough to throw yourself down a staircase and make it look good, but try throwing yourself down one and then hitting a tiny piece of tape at the bottom. It's tricky.

The other tricky thing was trying to do all this while acting. With all the focus on hitting those pieces of tape at exactly the right time, it was easy to forget about playing Sam's emotions. Besides, there was no one acting opposite me—I was acting and reacting based on what I knew Willy's character would do. But he wasn't there, so I was running around this set, yelling at nobody, swinging at nobody, throwing myself down stairs to grab nobody. It was a very strange experience.

Doing all that in the confines of a closed set was one thing, but doing it outside in front of a crowd of gawkers was another. We used the computerized camera technique for the scene where Sam follows Willy to his apartment building and then sees his former buddy Carl there. We shot those scenes up in Bedford-Stuyvesant, a rough part of New York that was even rougher back in 1989. Not a whole lot of movies get shot there, so a crowd of people had gathered around to watch.

This was a big, emotional turning point in the movie. It's

the first time that Sam realizes his own friend Carl was the one who set up his murder. Sam follows Carl out onto the street and swings wildly at him, furious and hurt at his friend's betrayal. It's a very intense moment.

I got really geared up for this scene, summoning all the emotion I could to convey Sam's hurt and anger, and when Jerry yelled "Action," I stormed out of Willy's apartment screaming and swinging. But of course, because we were shooting with the computerized camera so that Sam's punches would go right through Carl, I did this scene completely alone. There was no Carl there. So the crowd of people who'd gathered to watch just saw me coming out yelling and swinging like a maniac. And they started laughing.

Looking back, I'll admit that it probably looked pretty funny doing that scene alone. But at the time, I definitely didn't see any humor in it. I stopped and turned to the crowd, furious.

"Shut the fuck up!" I yelled, my adrenaline pumping from the emotion of the scene. "You want to get out here and do this yourself? You think this is easy?" People looked startled, but they shut up. And when we went back to shoot the scene again, you could hear a pin drop. Nobody made a peep until we finished the whole take. When Jerry yelled "Cut," the whole crowd broke into applause.

After we wrapped on *Ghost*, I did a 180-degree turn for my next role. I went from playing the straitlaced, Mr. Nice Guy banker Sam Wheat to the Zen-surfer-bank-robber Bodhi in *Point Break*.

Bodhi was a once-in-a-blue-moon character, the bad guy whom you love because you believe what he believes in—until he believes it too far and breaks the law and kills someone. I loved Bodhi because I identified with his quest for perfection and the ultimate adrenaline high. In fact, when I was first approached about *Point Break* years earlier, they asked me to play Johnny Utah, the FBI-agent-turned-surfer. But Bodhi was the only role for me. He's a complex character who can read people instantaneously and knows exactly how to play them. I couldn't wait to sink my teeth into that role.

I also was excited about getting paid to be a beach bum. *Point Break* is a surfing movie, so going to work meant hopping into my Range Rover at dawn, heading out to the beach, and being on a surfboard as the sun came up. Both Keanu Reeves and I got surfing lessons, but we had world-class stunt doubles for the really big waves. When you get out there in the ocean, you realize quickly that serious surfing takes huge amounts of both skill and courage.

To be a really good surfer, you have to start when you're a flexible little kid and have no fear, because you're trying to pop up on a wave that's lifting you higher and higher, sometimes up to the height of a three- or four-story building. Then, just at the moment you have to be functioning at your highest level, the fear kicks in, and you go over the top and get your brains pounded in. I had surfed in Galveston growing up, so I knew the basics, but this was different. Messing around in these big waves was dangerous, so I just focused on being able to paddle out, pop up onto the board, and do a cutback on the wave. I just wanted to be good enough so that when they cut from a shot of me to a shot of my surfer double, I didn't look like Bobby Darin on the soundstage of a fifties beach movie.

Keanu and I also got to skydive for *Point Break*. I had never done it before, even though my brother Donny had gotten seriously into skydiving. I knew it was only a matter of time before I decided to throw myself out of an airplane, too, and *Point Break* finally gave me the perfect opportunity to do it.

The funny thing was, the first time I jumped I felt no fear at all. I stood at that open airplane door looking down, knowing there was nothing between me and the ground but air. I should have been terrified. But it's such a sensory overload that I couldn't really take it all in, so I just jumped. It wasn't until the second jump that I suddenly found myself scared—because my brain had a chance to catch up and figure out what was going on. On the videotape of that second jump, I'm smiling, but you can see the jump master having to rip my hands off the bar to get me out the door.

The movie's insurers didn't want Keanu and me skydiving, even though they seemed to have no problem with us going out and getting pummeled by giant waves. I couldn't believe they were so shortsighted about it, since we were much more likely to get injured or die in those waves. I can't count how many times I ended up getting caught in an impact zone and sucking in water, unable to get up for air. But the insurers insisted that skydiving was just too dangerous, so we actually spent two days shooting skydiving footage after the film had officially wrapped.

That didn't include the big, climactic skydiving scene, though, because that one didn't really happen in midair. It couldn't have. For one thing, Keanu and I are supposedly talking to each other throughout a free fall, which is impossible. And he supposedly leaps out of a plane without a parachute, catches Bodhi, and the two of them successfully deploy Bodhi's chute and float down. This couldn't happen in real life either, as Johnny Utah would have flown right off him when Bodhi deployed the chute. So we shot the scene with giant rigger fans and a contraption that held us in place in midair, to look like we were falling.

With all the skydiving, surfing, chase scenes, and fight scenes, *Point Break* was one of the most fun movies I've ever worked on. It was also one of the most painful, as I cracked my left wrist and a couple of ribs, and tore up my shoulder and elbow. The worst injury didn't come while we were shooting, though. It came when I was bored out of my mind back at the trailers.

I'd been hanging around a parking lot all day, waiting to be called to shoot a scene. I walked over to the prop truck and said, "Hey, you guys got a skateboard?"

"Sure," said one of the guys, and grabbed one from the back. "Here you go," he said. "Don't kill yourself." I just laughed and said thanks, and then hopped on the board. It shot out from under me, and I fell straight down onto my elbow, which drove my arm bone right up into my shoulder, tearing tendons and my rotator cuff. I was dizzy with pain, but knew that if I let anyone know I was hurt, there would be repercussions with the movie's insurers. So I just acted as if everything was okay.

Whether I'm dancing, playing sports, acting, or anything else, I try never to allow pain to derail me. Pain is a constant companion when you make action movies. It's also just a part of living with a serious knee injury. But I learned how to put the pain elsewhere, how to compartmentalize what was happening in my body.

Pain is nothing more than a sensation, and you can choose to give in to it, or choose to control it. It's how I managed to sustain my career for this long, and even how I've managed to fight cancer. Pain, like fear, can even be your friend if you let it. It sharpens your focus, and lets you know you're alive.

But Lisa and I had to deal with another kind of pain during this period, one that had nothing to do with physical aches. This one had to do with heartache.

Lisa and I had been together for fifteen years now, and despite some ups and downs over that time, our relationship was strong. We both loved children and definitely wanted to have a family of our own. With my career going so well and both of us in our thirties, this was the perfect time to go for it.

To our excitement, Lisa got pregnant. I couldn't wait to become a dad, to have a child with this woman whom I loved so dearly. The idea of having a family together with her made me happier than anything. And I wanted to be the best father I could be—the kind of father my dad had been to me.

About three months into her pregnancy, Lisa went in for her latest ultrasound. She'd gone into the exam room before me, and by the time the nurse showed me in, the ultrasound had already begun. As soon as I walked into that room, I knew something was very wrong.

Lisa was crying. The technician still had the ultrasound wand on her belly, but she already knew the baby's heart wasn't beating. She didn't even have to say anything to me—one look at her face, and I knew the worst possible thing was true. "Oh, my God," I said, fighting to control my emotions. I looked from the ultrasound machine to Lisa's face and back, struggling to stay composed.

I felt completely crushed with grief. I'd been so excited that day, so thrilled at going in to see my baby's heartbeat. And he was dead. I couldn't handle it—when we got to the parking lot, Lisa and I both wept bitterly, holding each other tight. I grieved as I hadn't done in years, since my father died. Even now, neither of us can talk about that day without tearing up.

We wanted to try again, but the loss had been so devastating that we just couldn't do it right away. At that point, we figured we had plenty more years ahead of us. Eventually, we did start trying again, and we kept at it for many years, hoping Lisa would get pregnant again. But she never did.

When she became perimenopausal, our doctor told her we could try in vitro fertilization with a donor egg. But when Lisa suggested it to me, I knew I didn't want to do it. "I wanted it to be *us*," I told her, feeling the tears come again. And I really did. I wanted a child, but what I really wanted was to create a child with this amazing woman I loved.

We always knew we could adopt, and we talked seriously about it. While I was shooting a movie in Russia, Lisa even took a trip to a Russian orphanage to do some research on adopting there. But somehow, as the years went by, we never did it. I'm not sure either Lisa or I could even explain why, except to say that it must be tied somehow to the shock and grief of that terrible day in the doctor's office. But if there's one thing I regret in my life, it's that we didn't have children. It makes me sad for myself, but maybe even more so for Lisa, who would have been a beautiful mother.

# Chapter 12

After *Ghost* came out, the whirlwind started up again, fiercer than ever. The movie shot up to number one at the box office, and it stayed at the top for four weeks. The magazine and TV interviews and photo requests kept flooding in—our phone never seemed to stop ringing that year. It felt great to have such a good movie out, and Lisa was also having a blast, wrapping up her starring role in a TV show called *Super Force*, in which she played a police captain in the year 2020.

The tricky thing about success is, the more of it you have, the more you fear it will disappear. On the surface, we had everything we'd been fighting for all these years. My career was soaring, we had a beautiful ranch, and we had each other. I got nominated for my second Golden Globe Award for *Ghost*, and "Patrick Swayze" had become the household name my mother always believed it would be.

But what would come next? I was proud of my work in *Ghost*, and I desperately wanted to follow it up with another great role. This felt like my big chance—my best opportunity yet to vault myself into the company of serious, respected actors who get offered the best parts. If I could just keep this momentum going, maybe I wouldn't have to prove myself to Hollywood over and over and over again.

That's when I heard about the role of a lifetime, the chance to play an American doctor in Calcutta for one of the greatest directors in the business, Roland Joffé. The film was called *City of Joy*.

I had never met Roland Joffé before, but I'd seen his films, including *The Killing Fields* and *The Mission*. I knew he was incredibly passionate about his work and a man who never compromised on his vision. In fact, he was such a maverick that he rubbed some people in the business the wrong way—including reviewers, who seemed to love to tear his movies down. But I knew instinctively that the opportunity to work with him, on a movie that really explored the human condition, had the potential to change not only my career, but my life as well.

*City of Joy* is about an American doctor, Max Lowe, who becomes disillusioned and depressed after a young patient of his dies in surgery. He tries to escape his pain by traveling to India and losing himself there. To his surprise, he has a transformational experience, finding new meaning through helping Calcutta's poor.

I loved the character of Max. In fact, I identified with him. Max never felt he was good enough, and he was constantly battling his inner demons. I'd been doing the same ever since I was a boy in Texas, fighting those voices that always told me I had to try harder and be better than I was. Max's struggle was one I knew intimately, and I desperately wanted the chance to create his character onscreen.

I walked into the audition looking like a beach bum, with my hair and beard still bleached blond from *Point Break*. But Roland and I connected right away, and I opened up with him completely about how much this character and story meant to me. This wasn't like any other audition I'd been on—instead of reading for the part, Roland and I just talked. We forged a real bond that day, the foundation of a friendship that would last for life. He pushed me deep into exploring my own feelings, and I got very emotional as I tried to explain why I was so drawn to the part.

As Roland told me later, one thing in particular convinced him I was right for the role. It was the moment I told him, "If you will have me do this movie, I will work hard. But more than that, I will give you my heart." Roland operates on instinct, and at that moment, he knew he wanted me. He knew I would hold nothing back for this movie—and he also knew I'd need that kind of passion for what lay ahead.

But when Roland went to the producers and said, "We have to have Patrick Swayze for Max," the response was lukewarm. Despite the success of *Dirty Dancing* and *Ghost,* Hollywood still didn't see me as the kind of actor who could carry a serious drama. Some even still saw me as just "that dance guy." Roland didn't back down, though. He said, "It's Patrick. That's it. He *is* Max." Thanks to Roland's perseverance, I finally had the role I'd spent years hoping to get. So it was off to the black hole of Calcutta.


When Lisa and I arrived in Calcutta, the first thing we noticed was the thick, smoky fog that enveloped us as we walked out of the airport. We had never been to India before, so we didn't really expect to walk out into the hot night air to find the smog so thick you could barely see ten feet in front of you.

We loaded into a car, and the scene as we rode to our hotel

was surreal. There were a few streetlights, which cast some light through the darkness, but because of the soot in the air the light was diffused. So there was a strange eerie glow outside the car, with apparitions seeming to move in and out of the darkness. Women were dressed in flowing saris and men in loose-fitting cotton pants and shirts, and despite how late it was, there were people absolutely everywhere. Looking out the car windows, we felt like we were in another world.

As the driver navigated the crazy traffic of Calcutta we could see one cause of that choking smog. All along the roadways, poor Indians were cooking meals in open pots. The pots burned round patches of dried cow dung, the cheapest fuel available, which put out a pungent, thick smoke. Hundreds of millions of Indians cooked with these pots, contributing, along with coal smoke, to a massive cloud of black, sooty smog that hung over the country for months at a time.

Roland wanted to throw me right into the type of situation that Max Lowe found himself in. So the next morning, he took me straight to Mother Teresa's Home for the Dying—the place where the poorest of the poor Indians come to die.

Every country in the world has poor people, but the kind of poverty you see in India is staggering. Little children with spindly arms and legs, their eyes hollow from hunger. People missing arms and legs, their bodies covered with pus-filled sores. There's a level of desperation among the poor in India that I had never seen before, but there's a level of amazing spiritual richness, too. And Roland wanted me not just to see it, but to plunge into it—to care for the most destitute with my own hands, just as Max Lowe would do.

At Mother Teresa's, I did whatever the head nurse asked of me. When she saw that I wouldn't shy away from touching the sick, she put me to work with them. I washed the hands of a dying man, sat with a frail woman's head on my lap, helped clean up children who had soiled themselves. Yes, I was doing research for a movie—but this went way beyond that. It was impossible not to be touched by the incredibly deep need all around us. It humbled me, and made me realize once again how fortunate we are to have such comfortable lives.

The next stop was even more difficult. Roland took us to a street clinic, one of thousands across India that provide cheap medical services for people who have no money. There was a young boy, probably about eight years old, who came in for treatment while I was there. He had come in a couple of months earlier with badly burned arms, and the staff had bandaged them up. He was coming back because those bandages, now filthy, had grafted themselves into his skin. The boy was in a lot of pain, and those rotting bandages had to come off.

I took that little arm into my hands and began trying to pick out the putrid bandage threads. All I had to work with was saline water with some kind of milky antiseptic in it and a Swiss Army knife. His skin was raw and infected, but I just kept picking at that bandage. The boy could tell I was upset, so he even reached over himself to try to help, as if he were consoling me. He never shed one tear, which caused me to blink back tears myself. It took a couple of hours, but together we finally got the last remnants of that rotted bandage off.

The third stop of the day was a leprosy clinic in Titigar. Roland wanted to completely overload my senses, to put me in the place of this young, self-indulgent doctor who suddenly opens his eyes to the world around him. And he succeeded, because going to a leprosy clinic was definitely eye-opening for me.

We all sat down at a table with the head of the clinic, and before long a young man came in to serve tea. But when I saw a pair of fingerless hands gently placing my teacup in front of me, that was the moment I had to decide: Am I really in this or not? I didn't know anything about leprosy, and I had no idea if it was contagious or not. But to refuse the tea because of who served it would be beyond insulting. It would be rejecting everything I'd come here to do.

Roland and I looked at each other, and together we drank our tea. It was trial by fire: This was the moment I decided we were in this for better or for worse, the moment I totally committed to what we were doing here.

During the four months or so we were filming in Calcutta, we faced every conceivable obstacle. The shoot took place during the first Gulf War, so anti-American sentiment was running high. Huge crowds would gather outside my hotel, shouting for the American to go home. Protestors hurled homemade bombs onto the set, and although they were packed with harmless jute rather than projectiles that could kill or injure, it was still scary as hell to see one coming over the wall of the set. The producers hired more than a hundred Indian policemen to act as security, but more often than not they'd just slink into the crowd themselves if things got really rough.

From the beginning, Roland told all the Americans and British in the cast and crew that if we were asked, we should say we were from Canada or Australia. A few weeks in, when it became clear how aggressive the mobs were becoming, he held a meeting with all of us. "If you feel your life is in danger," he said, "you can go home with my blessing." There are a lot of directors who would bully everyone into staying no matter what happened, but Roland was far too decent and honorable a man to act that way. No one left. As the cast and crew took to saying, we were on a mission from God.

The Gulf War wasn't the only reason we were unpopular in Calcutta. The subject matter of Dominique La Pierre's best-selling book, *City of Joy*, which the movie was based on, was very controversial in India. Some felt that it showcased the absolute worst side of India and made the Westerner the hero. But Roland believed the story showed universal truths, that it got to the heart of what it means to be human and be connected as family. He believed strongly in the movie and was determined to make it, come hell or high water.

Roland had anticipated resistance in India, so he'd taken the precaution of building a giant set replicating a Calcutta slum. It was huge—five acres in all—and so realistic that when you see the movie, you can't believe it was actually shot on a set. It took eight weeks for hundreds of workers to create the shanties, trash-strewn alleys, and running sewers of the slum. And it was surrounded by a high wall with concertina wire on top, not only to keep out protestors, but to prevent Calcutta's poor from moving in.

It was filthy on the set, just like in a real slum, and for pretty much the entire shoot my clothes and skin were covered in dirt. We also battled "Delhi belly," which made me so sick I had to learn how to throw up and have diarrhea at the same time. (For the record, you sit on the toilet and throw up into the bathtub. I don't recommend it.) From the dirty water, I got conjunctivitis so bad I could hardly see, and I also accidentally got stabbed in the arm in one scene. I felt as if I *was* Max Lowe in this movie, feeling the shock of discovering India, and falling in love with it at the same time.

Coming back to the Oberoi Hotel after shooting was always

a strange experience. The hotel was a real oasis of luxury amid the poverty of India, and it always seemed amazing to come back to clean sheets and room service. But on the night when I settled in to watch the tape-delayed Academy Awards telecast, it felt even more surreal. Looking at all those Hollywood people dressed in their finery, with the women draped in millions of dollars of jewelry, felt bizarre.

Then came the moment that I'll never forget. Whoopi Goldberg won the Best Supporting Actress Oscar for her role in *Ghost*—the first time in almost fifty years that an African American had won the award. The audience went crazy as she made her way up to the stage, but then you could have heard a pin drop as she made her speech. It was very short—she thanked her family, Paramount, and Jerry Zucker, and then singled me out by name.

"I have to thank Patrick Swayze, who's a stand-up guy, who went to them and said, 'I want to do it with her,' " she said. Sitting there watching in my Calcutta hotel room, I was incredibly touched by Whoopi's unexpected thanks. It meant more to me than I could ever express.

The release date for *City of Joy* got pushed up by three months, as Roland's financial backers were anxious to make back their money. Roland had wanted that extra time to screen the movie and build the audience, but he didn't feel that he could say no to the people who'd made the film possible. So we ended up with a release date in April 1992.

Unfortunately, this was the month of the Rodney King verdict and the LA riots—the worst urban rioting since the assassination of Martin Luther King, Jr., in 1968. Los Angeles was soon gripped by a wave of looting and mayhem, and the mayor declared a curfew over the entire city. So just as this amazing film was hitting theaters, no one in LA could go see it. And across the rest of the country, people were glued to their TVs watching coverage of the riots, instead of going to the movies. *City of Joy* ended up doing weak business in its theatrical release.

I was beyond crushed. I really believed *City of Joy* was an amazing, uplifting movie that might possibly become a classic. Everything I'd hoped for had come true—Roland had brought out incredible performances, the camera work was fantastic, and the final cut was beautiful. When I finished work on *City of Joy*, it was the first time I ever really felt I'd done absolutely everything I could on a movie, to the very best of my ability. Seeing it fare worse than I'd hoped after all that was just heartbreaking.

And of course, I went straight to a very dark place, thinking that maybe it didn't do well because of me. The tremendous disappointment I felt over *City of Joy* tapped into every insecurity I still felt as an actor. No matter how obvious it was that external factors had played a big role at the box office, I couldn't shake the feeling that I had failed.

I called Roland the week after the film opened. "I hope you're not disappointed that you cast me," I said, my voice catching. He was such a good man, and such a great director, that I couldn't stand the thought that he might regret having offered me the role.

"Of course not, Patrick," he said in response. "I just hope you're not disappointed that I directed it."

Roland's answer was just what I needed to hear, but the good feeling didn't last long. I had put so much energy and passion into *City of Joy,* and I had dared to hope it would mark a turning point in my acting career. That it didn't do nearly as well as we'd hoped was devastating—even though the movie did change some minds about me in Hollywood, and the DVD sales are still strong. But the initial response sent me into a spiral that I didn't know how to get out of.

I hadn't been drinking very much over the previous year or so, having cut back after doing too much of it for too long. For a period of almost ten years after my father's death, I drank copious amounts of alcohol, mostly beer and wine but occasionally hard liquor, which really messed me up. Lisa had been concerned about my alcohol intake for a while, and we sometimes got into fights about it. So I had cut back significantly, and while I was in Calcutta I hardly drank at all.

But the disappointment over *City of Joy* threw me right back into a self-destructive place. I gave in to those demons that were forever trying to undercut me and spent a lot of time beating myself up for not being good enough, or successful enough. These feelings were so raw, so consuming, that I started sliding into serious depression, though I didn't realize it at the time. Adding alcohol was like pouring fuel on the fire. And did I ever pour it on.

The next movie I worked on after *City of Joy* was *Father Hood,* a drama about a wild man named Jack Charles who becomes a small-time hood. There were some interesting things about the character, and the director, Darrell Roodt, was fresh and talented. But compared to the kind of roles I'd hoped to get after *City of Joy,* this was a disappointment, even though the movie turned out to be good. Honestly, any role less than the caliber of Max Lowe would have been a disappointment.

What had long been the biggest frustration of my acting

career was peaking right now. Why couldn't I pull in the level of projects that I wanted, and that I seemed to have earned? I had done good work over the years, and had always tried to turn down junk. I had studied and explored and worked my ass off, and had believed in myself against all odds. But I just couldn't seem to break through. I can take a lot of pain and abuse, but if you get slapped around long and hard enough, the doubt just creeps in. You think, *Who am I fooling here? Maybe I'm just lying to myself.*

My character in *Father Hood*, Jack Charles, was darker than the ones I usually played. He does make the right decision at the end of the movie, but he's a desperado, on the run from the police. I've always had trouble dropping out of character after the director calls it a wrap at the end of the day, and this time was no different—as Lisa always jokes, "Please don't get cast as an axe murderer! I don't want you bringing that home!" So I was in the head of this bad guy all day and all night, which pushed me to darker and darker places.

I drank more while making *Father Hood* than I ever had before. One morning after a night of drinking, the crew had trouble waking me up. They were scared that I was slipping into a coma, but they knew that if someone called for an ambulance it would be instantly all over the news. They wanted to protect me, but what if I really needed medical help? I ended up being fine, but there were many mornings when I was slow to get going, hung over and already looking for a drink.

Lisa eventually had to ask Rosi, our assistant, not to tell her any more stories of what was happening on the set when she wasn't there. It was just too upsetting for her, especially since she knew there was nothing she could do. But when Lisa came to Las Vegas, the last location where we were shooting, to spend some time with me, she saw my most embarrassing moment of all. We were trying to shoot a scene in which I'm in the back of a car, but I'd had so much to drink, I kept passing out while the cameras were rolling.

For someone who takes so much pride in professionalism, this was about as low as it could get. I had never done anything like this, and I knew I was sacrificing my standards and integrity, but I just couldn't stop. Pretty much in one fell swoop, I managed to kill the fragile sense of self-worth and self-esteem I'd had after wrapping on *City of Joy*.

For Lisa, this was all incredibly agonizing to watch. She had tried everything she could think of, begging, arguing, fighting—but nothing worked. We got into terrible shouting matches, as our great passion for each other turned into intensely emotional fights. Tempers flared wildly and things got broken, and Lisa was almost ready to give up. Her survival instinct was kicking in, and she began turning from trying to save me to trying to take care of herself.

At the time, Lisa wasn't sure how to deal with what was happening to me, and to us. She was trying to change my behavior, without realizing that the only person who could change it was me. Negotiating and arguing and threatening don't work, though those are natural responses. But her actions had only been making things worse for both of us, to her frustration.

Everything came to a head when I returned home to LA after wrapping *Father Hood*. I walked in the door, and Lisa could see that I was drunk. She was sitting at the dining-room table with our friend Nicholas, and as she told me later, she turned to him and said, "I wish he'd just go back. I can't do this anymore."

Lisa didn't say anything to me about it that night. But the

next afternoon, when I woke up and came into the kitchen, she said, "Buddy, what are you planning to do?"

"What do you mean?" I said. "Why are you asking me this?"

"Because I need to know what I need to do," she said. The look in her eyes was as sad and serious as I'd ever seen. And I knew exactly what she was saying.

At that moment, I realized I wasn't as in control of my life as I thought. With drinking, I always believed I could stop when I wanted to. I'd always felt that alcohol wasn't the problem—the problem was the pain and insecurity that led me to drink. Alcohol was a symptom, not the disease itself. But looking at Lisa's face, I realized I had been in denial about what was happening, and how it was affecting her. And right then, I began to accept that I was helpless in the face of the emotional energy that drove me to that self-destructive behavior.

"I'm going to go someplace and get my shit together," I said to her. She knew I meant rehab, though I didn't think of it that way. I just knew I needed to go to a place where I could get help restoring myself. I needed help getting back the zest for life that I'd lost, to help keep me from spiraling down further.

Two days later, I checked in to a treatment facility in Tucson. At first, I was put off by the fact that they seemed to want to talk only about alcohol, because there were so many other underlying issues I needed to address. I also didn't like the feeling of being just another actor going to rehab—a victim, or a cliché. But after a month, I began to feel more in control. I began to take responsibility for my own life again, and the facility gave me the tools to do it.

One of the hardest things to realize is that taking responsibility is not the same thing as taking on guilt and blame. Saying "this is my fault" isn't taking responsibility; it's passing judgment on yourself. For me, taking responsibility meant figuring out what was wrong with my life that was causing me to drink. If I'm drinking for emotional reasons, that's when there's a problem. And taking responsibility means being aware of it and taking steps to curb it.

The other thing about rehab, and the reason so many people, including Hollywood celebrities, continue to have trouble afterward, is that it's not a quick fix—it just starts the process. It's like a muscle you have to exercise every day. Because if you really want to change, you have to want it every day.

After I got back to LA, I tried to keep all these things in mind. But what really helped me get back on track was starting to pursue a new dream. I had wanted to be a pilot all my life, and I decided to start taking flying lessons. When you fly an airplane, you're taking on all kinds of responsibility, so there is no room for wallowing in alcohol or allowing your demons to get the better of you. You have to study incredibly hard to get a pilot's license—it's like getting a college degree in a compressed time period. I threw myself into it, grateful to have a new challenge.

Once I began bouncing back from my drinking and depression, my relationship with Lisa began to heal. I joined her in New York, where she had been cast as one of the two female leads in *Will Rogers Follies* at the Palace Theater on Broadway. She played Ziegfeld's Favorite, and opened the show with a solo that showed off her beautiful voice and great charisma onstage. Lisa was thrilled to be starring on Broadway, and I was glad to be there for her—offering suggestions for her performance, running errands, and just generally being her cabana boy. We stayed in New York for six months, our first extended stay there since the late seventies. And we loved every minute of it.

In the meantime, I started looking again for good movie roles. Fortunately, the next role I got was a really fun one, playing a character named Pecos Bill in the Disney movie *Tall Tale*. Playing Pecos Bill allowed me to be a cowboy and ride horses all day, which was a balm for my soul. Any time I'm up in a saddle, the world around me just looks brighter. I had a hell of a lot of fun making that movie, and it brought me back into the hero role.

Little did I know it, but for my next big part, I'd be trading in that cowboy gear for a dress.

# Chapter 13

From the first time I heard about *To Wong Foo, Thanks for Everything! Julie Newmar*, I knew I wanted to be in it. It would be an amazing challenge to transform myself into a convincing woman, and playing a man in drag would really stretch me as an actor.

But once again, it was the same old story. Steven Spielberg was producing, and he wasn't keen on having me audition for the role. A lot of actors were being considered, including Johnny Depp, Tom Cruise, and Rob Lowe, but the part of Vida Boheme still hadn't been cast. I wasn't about to take no for an answer, so I got in touch with the director, Beeban Kidron, and told her I'd fly out to New York the next day for the audition if she would just see me. She agreed.

Before the audition at a loft downtown, I went to their makeup and wardrobe people to start the transformation into a woman. They gave me a dress and heels and a pretty little strawberry-blond cropped wig, and made up my face to look as feminine as possible. I had been trying out different mannerisms and voices, in an effort to seem like a real woman rather than a caricature, and I thought I'd hit on a pretty good tone. Now I was about to find out if anyone else would buy it.

I had read the script for the first time the night before, so when Beeban asked me to perform a two-page monologue, I told her I'd have to improvise.

"No, no, no," she said. "It has to be the words. You need to do the scene as it is in the script."

"I'll do the best I can," I told her, knowing that I'd have to improvise anyway, and that I needed to absolutely blow her and the producers away with it. "I may not have everything in the exact sequence, but i'll be close."

The monologue was Vida telling the story of her life, so what I did was take the details I remembered for her, and then insert some of my own. I told it from my own perspective: the story of Buddy Swayze's life if he'd grown up a drag queen in redneck Texas. I talked about getting beat up by five kids in junior high, and about getting teased by everyone at school. Everything I said was all true, except for the drag-queen part.

"There was nothing special about me," I said toward the end, my voice soft and low, "until I became a woman."

I don't think anyone in that room really expected that the guy from *Road House* and *Red Dawn* could really transform into a convincing woman. But by the end of my audition, I knew I had. It was so strange—I could tell from the energy in the room that people felt that I had really achieved becoming a woman. They didn't talk to me like I was Patrick Swayze. They talked to me like I was Vida Boheme.

After all the auditions were finished, Beeban narrowed the list to the ones she liked best, then took the tapes to Spielberg and the other producers. She didn't say who the actors were, but just invited them to watch the tapes and decide for themselves. Everyone agreed that I *was* Vida. But when Beeban revealed that it was actually me on that tape, no one could believe it—they were just blown away. I got the part, and just like that I was back in the game.

It takes a long time to turn a masculine man into a woman. First, you have to be incredibly well shaved, and not just on your face. All those places where men have hair and women don't—face, neck, even ears—have to be smooth as a baby's butt. Then, because men's pores are bigger than women's, the makeup department would apply a stuccolike filler, to smooth out your skin.

Then comes the makeup. You'd get a base coat of foundation, followed by powder. Lipstick, eyeliner, eyeshadow, fake eyelashes—the makeup artists are turning you into not just any woman, but a beautiful, glamorous woman. And my makeup guy on *Wong Foo* certainly knew something about that. He was Roy Helland, Meryl Streep's makeup man. And at about six feet five inches tall, he'd once been a towering, gorgeous drag queen himself.

Makeup usually took about three hours, after which my costars Wesley Snipes and John Leguizamo and I would go to the wardrobe room. I learned very quickly not to let them dress me in any cute little tight pantsuits, because that meant I'd have to use the assistance of an apparatus called the gender bender. This is a special piece of equipment, designed by some sadistic bastard with a sense of humor, which you tuck your manly parts into to make them "disappear." In reality, the gender bender pushes everything back in the other direction, between your legs. And yes, it's every bit as uncomfortable as it sounds.

When the wardrobe guys first explained how the gender bender worked, I said, "You want me to do *what*?" But this was part of the deal, so I went ahead and rearranged everything down there, as I was asked. While wearing it, you essentially spend the day sitting on your member. It's a very scary sensation after you do it for a long time, because your tallywhacker goes quite numb. And when that happens, you start to worry it's going to fall off. So very quickly I learned to ask for lovely little dresses that allowed my manhood to remain in its rightful place.

I never knew how many categories of drag queen there were until we started doing research for *Wong Foo*. And by "research," I mean going out to clubs with some of the most beautiful, statuesque, amazing queens I had ever seen. They were our "guides" to the drag world, and they showed us more than we ever knew existed.

We rented a huge limo, and John, Wesley, Lisa, the drag queens, and I hit all the Manhattan hotspots. We saw "royal court" queens, with their super-high-end couture gowns, and over-the-top comic drag queens, with huge hair, shaved eyebrows, and glittered eyelashes. There were drag queens who went for absolute authenticity, who looked exactly like women. And there were the down-on-their-heels drag queens who hung out in the seedy clubs by the waterfront and the piers by the Hudson River.

The level of talent in the drag world is phenomenal. These people could sing, they could dance, they could vamp. Some of the men singing as women had the most beautiful female voices I'd ever heard. We had a blast exploring their world, hanging out with women with fantastic names like Candis Cayne and Miranda Rights. And Lisa was pleased to get a compliment herself, when a drag queen passed her on the street, looked her up and down, and said, "Beautiful!"

Spending time with these men was incredibly eye-opening. Not only did they have an amazing sense of humor, they also had amazing courage. It takes *cojones* to be exactly who you are, especially when it's so different from what society has dictated for you. These drag queens weren't afraid to be exactly who they were, and to expect the rest of the world to catch up. It was inspiring to see.

I loved working with John and Wesley, both of whom looked absolutely fabulous in drag. We had a lot of fun during filming, though occasionally John's hyperactive energy started to drive me a little crazy. He's got only one speed—full throttle—and sometimes it got to be too much. But it did lead to one of the funnier moments on the shoot.

I'd made a quick trip back to LA the day before, and then flown all night to get back for an early-morning call on the set. When I arrived, I was completely exhausted and just wanted to get our rehearsal done. But John was in typical high-energy form, cracking jokes and doing his whole improv comedy routine. Normally, I found him hilarious. This particular morning, I wanted to stuff a sock in his mouth.

On and on he went, interrupting the rehearsal with one crazy comic riff after another. Finally, completely fed up, I snapped, "Oh, God! Would you just shut the fuck up for once?"

Well, John is a scrappy little fiery Latino who can probably kick the butts of guys three times his size. He came right at me, fists up, yelling, "Come on, let's go! You want to fuck with me? I'll fuck you up!"

The two of us stood there, yelling insults in each other's faces, our chests puffed out like a couple of roosters. But the funny thing was, we had forgotten we were dressed in half-drag. Both John and I were wearing stocking caps, makeup and eyelashes, and garter belts—we must have looked ridiculous, a couple of tough guys ready to go at each other while wearing panty hose. I love John, and I love that he went at me with fists up and makeup on. Not many guys would have done that, and though it didn't seem funny at the time, it sure does now.

My goal in playing Vida was to be absolutely convincing as a woman. I worked hard at it, but I really enjoyed it, too. As a man, it was a fascinating exercise to get so closely in touch with my feminine side, and to see how differently people responded to me. In the end, I think I did make a pretty convincing woman. I wouldn't have slept with me, but I know a lot of guys who would have, and not just at closing time.

Once I started dressing in drag, Lisa occasionally found me eyeing her clothes. "Girlfriend," she said, "you stay away from my closet!"

"I'm not interested in your clothes," I sniffed back, with Vida's quiet indignation. "Just your accessories."

I really didn't mind wearing women's clothes as long as the gender bender wasn't involved. But Wesley absolutely hated it. When we wrapped *Wong Foo*, he held a ceremonial funeral for his gender bender, wig, and clothes. He burned them and buried the ashes in the Nebraska soil, relieved to be free of them. But I liked my clothes, and even asked Lisa if she wanted any of them after the shoot was over. She just laughed and said, "Buddy, you do realize we're not the same size, don't you?" In the end, she took a one-size-fits-all Armani shawl—the only thing that would fit her.

*Wong Foo* went to number one on its opening weekend, but in the end it didn't do as well as we had hoped. The reviews were mostly good, and the legendary reviewer Gene Siskel loved my performance and even predicted an Oscar nomination for me. I didn't get one, but I did receive my third nomination for a Golden Globe Award. That was incredibly validating, because I'd really pushed myself to become Vida, to get to the place where I'd look at myself in the mirror and think, "Now, there's a woman." I loved Vida, and even missed her a little bit when she was gone.

Lisa and I both enjoyed the *Wong Foo* shoot, and my career was again on an upswing. But personally, that period marked the beginning of a difficult time, starting with two terrible, tragic deaths in our lives. It started with my older sister, Vicky, who committed suicide in December 1994.

Vicky was four years older than me, and she and I were close as kids even though we fought like cats and dogs. She was incredibly talented—a beautiful dancer and singer, and an amazing actress. Vicky had the same pressure on her as all the Swayze kids, to be the best and push the hardest, but as an adult she also had another burden to bear. She suffered from depression, and was eventually diagnosed as bipolar.

Vicky's struggle with depression was long and intense. She had gotten married and had kids, but when her demons kicked in, she'd take off and disappear for long stretches of time. Like many families of bipolar people, we suffered through her terrible times and never knew what to expect when we saw her. Sometimes, she would come to see us and give vent to the anger within her, or she'd leave heartrending messages on our answering machine. We weren't sure how to deal with Vicky's pain, and although we tried our hardest to support her, both emotionally and financially, it never felt as if we did enough. But the sad truth was, nothing would have been enough.

Vicky's doctors had prescribed a variety of medications, which she hated taking. About two years before she died, we found her a doctor who specialized in getting people off psychiatric drugs. The terrible irony was that although this really seemed to help, and Vicky felt better than she had in years, it ended with her killing herself.

As her doctor explained to us, it was possible that switching medications allowed Vicky to get just well enough to see how horrible she really felt her life was, which made me feel as if our efforts to help had actually triggered her death. The fact that she'd died was devastating enough, but because she'd killed herself, all I could think was, could I have saved her? Did I do enough? I felt so much guilt, it began to throw me into a depression of my own. I just couldn't shake the feeling that I was somehow responsible.

Vicky's suicide really rocked my world, and not just because of the guilt I felt. It made me wonder how much of her was also in me. Being a Swayze is a gift and a curse, because we all do possess this kind of wild Irish temperament. That temperament unleashes powerful things in terms of creative work, but it can be an enemy as well as a tool. You have to keep it in balance to survive, and Vicky hadn't been able to do that. I think all of us Swayze kids felt vulnerable about ourselves after her suicide.

Yet despite my own self-destructive streak, I've always had an even stronger urge for self-preservation. No matter how much despair I've felt in any given period, even during my absolute lowest lows, I never came close to considering suicide. Part of the reason is that I have a strong optimistic streak—deep down, I always believe things will get better somehow. But Vicky's death seriously battered that optimism. For the first time in my life, dark feelings of cynicism began to creep in.

I had never allowed myself to feel like a victim before. But it was hard not to feel, sometimes, that no matter what you do, life is going to smack you down. No matter how hard I tried, no matter how good a person I tried to be, bad things kept happening. I never admitted it to anyone, and I never stopped pushing ahead, but for the first time I started feeling that I couldn't get a break. And then, as if to prove my point, things got even worse.

Not long after Vicky's death, our beloved 140-pound Rhodesian Ridgeback, Cody, died. Cody was more than a dog to me—he was like my son, my guardian warrior, my conscience. He was a beautiful, special animal who'd been by my side since he was a puppy. And his death, coming on the heels of Vicky's, just devastated me.

Cody had been with us through all the ups and downs of our lives for the past thirteen years. He was with me when I was a struggling young actor on the set of *Red Dawn,* and he was our protector when fame started changing our lives. The bond he and I shared was deeper than I had with anyone except for Lisa. When he was diagnosed with cancer, both Lisa and I were so crushed, we got him every treatment we could and begged for him to hang in there.

And he did, for a whole year. Cody willed himself to stay alive for us, as he knew how desperately we wanted him to live.

I learned so much about the struggle to live from him. When he started getting treatment, he went back to being his old self for a while. But the disease eventually caught up to him, and when he hit his next bad stretch we knew we had to let him go. Lisa and I held him in our laps as he took his last breath, and although I knew his spirit was free, I felt an incredibly deep sadness that he wouldn't be here with us anymore.

When those you love die, the best you can do is honor their spirit for as long as you live. You make a commitment that you're going to take whatever lesson that person or animal was trying to teach you, and you make it true in your own life. Their having been in your life changed you in some beneficial way, and making that commitment is the only way you can ease the pain of their absence. But more than that, it's a positive way to keep their spirit alive in the world, by keeping it alive in yourself. I've tried to honor that with my father, my sister, Cody—with anyone we've loved who has passed on.

With everything that had happened over the previous couple of years, Lisa and I started to seriously reevaluate how we were living our lives. For too long, we'd been running in the whirlwind, taking on too many things at once and ignoring the needs of our spirits. Together, we decided to simplify things, to get back to the basics.

At its peak, our horse business—showing and breeding—had included fifty horses, the majority of which we kept in Texas. This was way more than we could be personally involved with, so we sold some and cut back on traveling to horse shows. We also got rid of some of the clutter that we'd been collecting at Rancho Bizarro. And we decided to focus more on the things that made us happy, rather than the things that ended up controlling our lives instead of enriching them. But the biggest thing we did, by far, was to finally fulfill a lifelong dream of owning a real ranch.

Ever since we'd spent time in New Mexico during the shooting of *Red Dawn*, Lisa and I had been in love with the rugged beauty and fresh air of the mountains there. In the late 1990s, we had an opportunity to purchase almost fifteen thousand acres of gorgeous ranch land, near where we'd filmed *Red Dawn*. It was like buying a piece of heaven, so we jumped at the chance.

For me, this was the fulfillment of a vow I'd made back when my dad was alive. I was sorry he wasn't here to be a part of it, but I was proud to be returning to my cowboy roots, just as he'd always hoped I would.

With thousands of acres of pine trees, scrub brush, sparkling rivers, and gently sloping meadows, Lisa and I could explore to our hearts' content. And we did, every chance we got—running horses through the brush, camping out for weeks at a time, learning every square foot of that beautiful ranch. I got to test my survival skills once again, living off the land and being as close to nature as a man can get.

Lisa and I were now both pilots, so we could fly ourselves back and forth to New Mexico. And we did, every chance we got. Because being out in nature, out at the ranch we loved, always helped restore our spirits in trying times.

In May 1998, I was shooting a scene for the film *Letters from a Killer*, when disaster struck.

It was late afternoon, and we were trying to get a few final shots for a big chase scene. My character, Race Darnell, is riding a horse bareback, galloping through the forest with the

FBI in hot pursuit. The scene called for me to race my horse right under a diagonally growing oak tree, right by a camera. A small crowd of people had gathered near the tree to watch the action—but they were standing in the path my horse would be racing down. Several hundred yards away, as I waited for my cue to come over the walkie-talkie, I had no idea they were there.

When the director yelled "Action," I spurred my horse to a gallop. We raced toward the tree, but where I needed the horse to go right, to match the previous shot, he wanted to go left. He'd seen the people milling around, blocking his path, and he didn't want any part of it. When he started going left, I had to quickly pull him right again, or the shot would be ruined.

Everything happened in an instant. I pulled the horse sharply back to the right, and he cut like a stick of dynamite— he changed directions so fast that I just flew right off his back. The only thing that saved me from crashing headfirst into that oak tree was instinct: In a split second, I grabbed his mane with both hands and flipped myself over, smashing into the tree legs-first.

The sound was like a two-by-four snapping in half. The impact broke both my legs and tore tendons in my shoulder, and I collapsed to the ground. I didn't know right away how badly hurt I was, but I knew something was wrong, since I could feel a strange pressure in my right thigh.

My longtime stunt double, Cliff McLaughlin, was at my side in a flash. He heard me say, "Let me just walk it off. I'll be okay"—the same thing I'd said on that high school football field nearly thirty years earlier. But I wasn't going to be walking away from this accident. I tried to sit up, but I could feel myself going into shock, which was incredibly dangerous out here in the woods with the nearest hospital miles away. I lay back down and tried to move my legs, and that's when I finally realized my right femur had snapped in half.

The set medic wanted to strap my legs together with oak branches and drive me in a Chevy Suburban to UC Davis, about fifty miles away. "Hell, no," I told him. "Do not touch my legs." I had a GPS device and a radio that could communicate with air traffic, which would help a medevac helicopter locate us out here in the boonies. We made the emergency call, gave the coordinates, and talked the chopper pilot in to our location, but it still took them over an hour to get to us.

Meanwhile, I was lying under that tree in agony. I willed myself not to think about the pain, but it came in ever-intensifying waves, until it was absolutely blinding. My broken femur was resting on my femoral artery. Luckily for me, it hadn't actually punctured that artery—if it had, I would have bled to death in minutes. I tried not to move, even as the pain grew even more searing. It felt like an eternity before the helicopter arrived, but that wasn't the end of the ordeal by far.

The medical guys on the chopper tried to put my leg into a traction splint, but they had the bone out of alignment. As they tightened the splint, I could feel something was very wrong, but I was still afraid of moving too much since the bone was on my artery. It was an excruciating few minutes, but I finally hoisted myself up and readjusted my weight. Despite the intense pain this maneuver caused me, I managed to get the bone aligned properly.

Lisa didn't see the accident, but she got there quickly after it happened. She was worried, of course, but also upset with me for having been riding at all. Cliff had been ready to jump in as my stunt double, but I'd told him to relax, as I really wanted to do the scene myself. I couldn't think of anything more fun than shooting through the woods bareback on a horse—it was the kind of thing I loved to do, and here I was getting paid to do it.

But Lisa had another reason for not wanting me to ride: I had come off that same horse just the day before, while rehearsing for the scene. In that accident, I had torn some tendons in my shoulder, and had even gone to the hospital to get it checked out. With my shoulder hurt, I shouldn't have been riding at all the next day. "Let Cliff earn his money!" Lisa told me. But I was stubborn. And now I had two broken legs to show for it.

The funny thing—and believe me, there weren't many funny things about this accident—was when the set medic called the hospital to say, "Patrick Swayze's had a horse accident and is coming in," they replied, "Yeah, we saw him already. He was in here yesterday." He had to explain that I'd come off the horse again, and that this time it was more serious.

By the time the medevac helicopter got me to the hospital, the pain was unbearable. The doctors went right at it, giving me pain medication, CAT scans, the works. Luckily for me, the hospital at UC Davis had the world's foremost expert on a new way to treat femur breaks. It used to be that anyone who broke a femur had to have the leg split open and go through months of healing time. But this new technique required only a small incision and a long drill bit, which meant you didn't have to heal muscles that had been sliced open. Three hours after surgery, the doctors had me get up and walk. And three months later, I was back at work, which would have been unheard-of even a few years earlier.

But even though my physical wounds healed quickly, other wounds did not. This was the first accident I'd ever had that really came close to killing me. If I hadn't managed to flip myself over the horse, I'd have gone into that tree headfirst. I would either have been killed instantly or have broken my neck and been left paralyzed, as Christopher Reeve had been not so long before. I'd done some crazy stunts on horses, but this accident made me realize that no matter how good a rider you are, when you're riding bareback on a horse, you're nothing but a human projectile.

It was as if the invisible shield that had always protected me had finally broken. I'd always acted as if I were invincible, because I always felt invincible. Now, with a shock, I realized I wasn't. I had always made fear work for me. But now fear was getting the better of me. There's a line I say in *Point Break* that really rings true: Fear causes hesitation, and hesitation causes your worst fears to come true. I had never been hesitant before, but now I was.

I had nightmares where I'd see myself flying off the horse and smashing into that tree. I'd wake up in a sweat, my heart beating like crazy and fear coursing through me. It got so bad that at one point, I even went to a doctor who specializes in treating post-traumatic stress disorder. I had to find a way to get over the fear that was paralyzing me, but I didn't know how.

With time, I was able to get back the courage the accident stole from me. I went back to doing everything on horses I'd done before the accident, and loving it. And the nightmares stopped. But even now, when I remember the feeling of hurtling toward that tree, my heart starts pumping again. Even with all the movie stunts I'd done, that was the first time I'd had a real brush with death.

Less than two years later I'd have another, even more dramatic brush with death. And for that one, I still don't know to this day how I survived.

# Chapter 14

I n early May 2000, after a particularly dry spring, the National Park Service set a controlled fire in northern New Mexico to burn off brush and grass. For months, the area had suffered record-setting high temperatures, and the landscape was as parched as it had been in decades. So when fierce winds suddenly whipped up the flames, the fire quickly got out of control. Within days, huge swaths of New Mexico were ablaze.

Lisa and I were at Rancho Bizarro in Los Angeles, but we became more and more worried as we watched the news coverage of the wildfires. Tens of thousands of people were being evacuated, and their homes were going up like tinder. News reports showed walls of flames and fleeing residents, and President Clinton declared a state of emergency in several New Mexico counties. All I could think was that our beautiful ranch—our haven and spiritual home—was in danger.

We sweated things out in LA for a couple of weeks, but as the fire drew closer to our ranch, I knew I had to do something. I couldn't just sit thousands of miles away as the place I loved went up in smoke—it wasn't the Swayze way to sit idly by when action might help. When we heard the authorities were evacuating the canyon where our house was, that was the last straw. I decided to fly out there and get into the canyon somehow, to at least bulldoze a fire break around our house.

Late on the night of May 31, I told Lisa I was flying to New Mexico the next morning. "You're what?" she said. "Buddy, they're evacuating the canyon. You won't even be able to get near the ranch." By now, I was operating more on emotion than on logic, but I couldn't just stay put. All I knew was, if I stood aside while that raging fire destroyed our ranch, I'd never forgive myself for not having done something.

Lisa tried to convince me not to go, but I was determined. Because I was at an emotional fever pitch, I hardly slept, and before the sun rose, I threw some clothes into a bag and headed out to the Van Nuys airport. I settled into the cockpit of our Cessna 414a to make the three-hour flight to New Mexico just before dawn broke.

About a month earlier, Lisa had encountered a dangerous situation while flying the Cessna near the Grand Canyon, where she'd come to visit me on the set of *Waking in Reno*. Lisa had taken up flying at my urging, after initially not being all that interested. But when she started taking lessons, she loved it, and she even learned how to do aerobatics—doing flying loops and other stunts in the air. She got so good that when she entered aerobatics competitions, she placed ahead of instructors who were competing. She was—and still is—an experienced, coolheaded pilot.

She had been climbing to a higher altitude, when all of a sudden, she heard a screaming noise in the cockpit. The noise startled her, but she quickly realized that the noise meant the cabin wasn't pressurizing properly as she climbed. An outflow valve was stuck, inhibiting the free flow of air—the squealing was like the noise a balloon makes when you slowly leak air out of the neck. We had a bad habit of occasionally smoking in the cockpit, and the sticky residue on the outflow valve was a result of tar from cigarettes.

Luckily, she was losing pressurization slowly, so she had time to come down to a safe altitude. Otherwise, she'd have been in big trouble. When an airplane's cabin isn't pressurized properly, there's not enough oxygen, which leads to hypoxia and possibly death. That's exactly what happened to the golfer Payne Stewart, who died along with five other people when the Learjet they were flying in lost pressurization. The pilots passed out and eventually died from lack of oxygen, and the plane just kept on flying for several more hours until it finally ran out of fuel and crashed. Fortunately, Lisa realized quickly what was happening, so she was able to descend to a safe altitude and finish her flight. And we got the plane serviced right after the incident.

On the morning of June 1, I decided to fly at a relatively low altitude—thirteen thousand feet—in case the pressurization problem recurred. I brought the Cessna to thirteen thousand feet, set the autopilot, and settled in for the rest of the flight. And that's the last thing I remember, until suddenly becoming aware of green and brown around me, and everything spinning. I looked around for blue sky and tried to aim for it. But the plane was at a very low altitude, and when I saw a strip of pavement with a strange oval at one end, one thought managed to penetrate the fog in my brain: *That must be the airport.*

I hooked a hard left to line up with what I thought was the runway. The next thing I knew, there were electrical power boxes in front of me, and I vaguely remember trying to push the plane over or around them. Then suddenly, I was on the ground. I sat stunned for a moment in the cockpit. I was so groggy and disoriented, it didn't feel like whatever had just happened was real. But when I turned around and saw our two dogs, Boda and Jazz, wagging their tails in the cabin of the airplane, I knew it must be.

I opened the plane's door and stepped down onto the street, still thinking I was in New Mexico. I had no idea that I'd just had an off-airport landing, or that my airplane was damaged. In fact, I had just landed on the street of what was to become a new housing development in Prescott Valley, Arizona. It was just being constructed at the time, so there was hardly anyone around to see my plane descend, clip two light poles and a power box, and still somehow land without crashing.

A couple of construction workers came running over, and I vaguely remember one of the guys telling me I'd clipped something on the way down. I walked around the front of the plane to look at the wing, and when I saw that it was damaged, I got upset for the first time—this plane was Lisa's and my baby, and I'd hurt it. I still didn't understand the enormity of what had happened, but little by little, the truth started penetrating the fog of my hypoxia-addled brain.

The first thing I did was call Lisa—a call I dreaded making, as I knew she'd be upset. "Lisa, I've had an off-airport landing," I told her. "I thought I was landing in New Mexico, but I ended up in a housing development in Prescott, Arizona. I'm okay, but the plane is damaged."

As Lisa told me later, she just went numb as I told her what happened. It was almost too much for her to take in, after the difficulties we'd been dealing with over the past few years.

What made it worse was the fact that hypoxia slurs your speech, so it sounded as if I'd been drinking. This effect wore off quickly, but because I called Lisa so soon after landing, all she knew was that I'd damaged the plane in an unscheduled landing, had nearly killed myself doing it, and on top of it sounded as if I was unfit to fly.

The next call I made was to the Federal Aviation Administration, to report the incident. I described what had happened, and the FAA representative told me he'd call the National Transportation Safety Board. So all the official wheels were in motion for dealing with the incident. Then, I made a decision that seemed sensible at the time, but that created its own problems.

I was carrying some beer and wine on board, which was of course legal—Lisa and I often brought food and drink from LA to New Mexico, since it was a long drive from the ranch to the nearest store. I should have just left it where it was, but instead I gave it to the construction workers. There was no doubt that photographers were on the way, and I had a feeling that if word got out there was alcohol on board, they'd try to twist the story into "Patrick Swayze Flies Drunk." I was trying to minimize possible complications, but when the story came out that I'd gotten rid of the alcohol, people assumed I was trying to cover something up.

I was anxious to get away from the scene before photographers showed up, so I asked one of the construction workers to give me a ride to a hotel, where I could settle in and take care of things. Lisa and our longtime flight instructor, Frank Kratzer, joined me there as soon as they could, and we waited for the National Transportation Safety Board investigators to arrive at the site, so we could meet with them and answer any questions they had.

The NTSB investigation later revealed that a clamp on the hose connecting the plenum chamber to the upper plenum had malfunctioned. That alone would have been enough to cause a pressurization problem, but the situation was also exacerbated by two other factors: the continued presence of tar deposits on that rubber outflow valve, and the fact that I was a heavy smoker. When you have a three-pack-a-day habit, as I had at the time, your lungs don't function as well at altitude as those of nonsmokers. The NTSB report noted that the combination of all these factors meant I almost certainly had become hypoxic during the flight. And it found no evidence of alcohol as a factor.

But the really scary thing was this: Nobody wakes up from full-on hypoxia. Once you have passed out due to lack of oxygen in the brain, it's impossible to recover unless you descend to a breathable altitude. I had apparently stopped responding to air traffic control around Needles, California, near the Arizona state line. Yet somehow, I must have knocked off the autopilot between there and Prescott Valley, which allowed the plane to descend. Otherwise, my plane would have just continued at thirteen thousand feet, flying until it ran out of fuel, like Payne Stewart's plane. And I would have been dead.

Even though I'd stopped responding, my aircraft kept on flying. Air traffic control radar showed that between Needles and my landing in Prescott Valley, I almost hit the ground eleven times. I flew between 6,500 and 11,500 feet, narrowly missing the mountains. And my route looked like a strand of spaghetti, looping around with no purpose for about forty-five minutes.

Fortunately, as I approached Prescott Valley, my plane had gently drifted lower until there was enough oxygen in the air to revive me. I woke up at just a couple hundred feet above the ground and managed to land safely anyway. It was nothing short of a miracle. Robert Crispin of the NTSB even said to me, "This is the first time I've ever gotten to talk to a pilot who's suffered hypoxia." Pilots just don't live through that. But somehow, I had.

There was a lot of fallout from the off-airport landing. For one thing, Lisa and I never smoked in the cockpit again. I also offered to make a public-service announcement for the FAA, warning of the dangers of smoking while flying, which weren't widely known at the time.

Even though the problem had been mechanical, I still had to fight to keep my pilot's license, going through psychological testing and skills tests. That, combined with the repairs our plane required, meant it would be two more years before we could fly it again. But getting into the cockpit again wasn't nearly as tough as getting through the nightmares I began having regularly after the incident. I woke up many nights in a cold sweat, dreaming I was heading for a crash or floating aimlessly in the sky, unconscious to the end. Once again, I'd cheated death, but as with the horse accident on *Letters from a Killer,* this incident left painful scars that were hard to heal.

Lisa had a hard time coming to terms with it, too. She later told me that when I first called her from Prescott, her heart felt as heavy as a stone. We had been together twenty-five years by now, through thick and thin, through enough pain and joy to fill a hundred lifetimes. She hadn't wanted me to fly that morning in the first place, but when I did, and then nearly died doing it, she felt betrayed that I'd risked everything we'd built together—everything she loved. Lisa felt helpless and angry, and it would take some time for those feelings to subside.

This airplane incident, combined with my feelings of vulnerability after the horse accident, really messed with my head. I had cheated death once again—but what for? What was the point of all this? What was I adding to the world? My career was at a crossroads, and the past few years had shown me the darker side of fame. As high as my career had soared with the success of *Dirty Dancing* and *Ghost*, it just felt that much worse to be back struggling again.

Earlier in my life, I had made it through difficult times by always focusing on the next dream. From football to gymnastics to dancing to acting, I always was able to throw myself fully into my next goal, and keep myself going. I never doubted that there was something great around the corner, and I never tired of pushing myself toward it.

But now I was starting to feel not just tired, but disillusioned, too. Had all this effort and pain been worth it? Had I created anything of value? As my relationship with Lisa frayed from the stress of constantly trying to prove myself, and struggling with feelings of never being quite good enough, I wondered if I had been focusing on the wrong things all along, to the detriment of what really mattered in life.

And even as I kept pushing to find good projects in Hollywood, the whole business of making movies was changing. With the economic downturn of 2000–2001, financing for bigger projects dried up and independent films started becoming more popular. There seemed to be fewer movies in general, and not as many good roles to choose from. It was tough going, but I did manage to shift gears and get roles in a few good independent films—*Green Dragon* with Forest Whitaker, *Donnie Darko* with Jake Gyllenhaal, and *Waking Up in Reno* with Billy Bob Thornton, Charlize Theron, and the beautiful Natasha Richardson among them.

There was one film both Lisa and I longed to make, but we'd spent years trying to pull it together without success. Ever since our play *Without a Word* had been a hit in the LA theater world back in 1984, we had wanted to turn it into a film. *Without a Word* had only a month-long run in LA, but even all these years later, people still stopped Lisa and me on the street to say how much they'd loved it. They would tell us how inspired they were, and how moved by the depiction of people who never gave up chasing their dreams. And they would ask us to please make a movie out of it.

If movies were made through sheer effort alone, we'd have finished this one long ago. Over the past two decades, Lisa and I had done everything possible to try to bring *Without a Word* to the screen. But there are so many factors that have to come together to make a movie, it's like herding cats, and we just couldn't seem to get all the cats together at once.

Early on, Lisa had done a full rewrite, since the play was nonlinear and would be hard to adapt for film without a more traditional narrative story line. We had entered into discussions with a variety of possible producers, financiers, directors, and writers, but for one reason or another, we were having trouble finding the right blend. We'd start down one road, thinking we were making progress, but then the project would fall apart.

A lot of the difficulty stemmed from the fact that the artistic vision Lisa and I had for the film was different from the vision other possible partners had. *Bagdad Cafe* director Percy Adlon wanted to direct at one point, but we parted ways when we couldn't agree on how the script should be structured. Pulitzer Prize–winning writer Israel Horowitz wrote several script drafts, but they weren't true to the spirit of the original piece. Lisa and I even had a falling-out with Nicholas Gunn, who had cowritten the play with us back in 1984, over differences about the movie script. We didn't speak for three years, though he eventually did rejoin our effort to make the film.

The project stalled again after Nicholas left, until we realized it was do-or-die time. Lisa and I knew we wouldn't be able to do the film's very demanding dance sequences forever, so we had to make it happen soon—or let it go. Nicholas came back, and we had an associate producer on board. But we were still having problems finding a writer who could deliver the script we wanted.

And that's when Lisa really stepped up. She invited Nicholas and the producer, Janice Yarbrough, who had run our production company at Fox, to dinner. With all four of us at the table, she said, "I've got the burn. I have to do this script. I know what needs to be done, and I can write it."

A dead silence fell at the table, and I looked at Lisa. Her face showed a kind of determination I'd never seen before, and although it was clear that Nicholas and Janice weren't convinced she was the best choice, she wouldn't back down. She'd always been the type to defer to others, playing down her own skills. But not this time. She'd worked on nearly all my movie scripts over the years, and had written a theatrical musical, so she was completely prepared for the task. More important, she knew the story in her bones.

In the face of their obvious reticence, Lisa said, "I lived this. I know it better than anyone, and I can write it better than anyone." As she spoke, I saw in her eyes that she was absolutely right, and I suddenly knew with every fiber of my being that she could do it. I made up my mind at that moment to support her no matter what, because she'd earned this and would do it better than anyone.

Janice threatened to quit, but Lisa stood her ground. And even though Janice did end up walking away from the project, Lisa knew it was just a difference of professional opinion, and we remained friends with Janice. Lisa never wavered, and in addition to writing the script, she took on the director's duties, too. She had directed several professional videos about horses and aircraft, and had studied the craft seriously with directors and cinematographers on numerous film sets over the years. Lisa knew what she was doing—and now she was stepping up for herself to have the chance to do it.

This was the film that finally led Lisa to put herself out there in a way she'd long been reluctant to. It was a huge turning point professionally, and I was thrilled for her—and for our movie.

Lisa was excited about taking on the roles of writer and director, but she felt that trying to do both, and act in the film, too, might be too much. "Lisa," I told her, "you've got to do this role. It's in your DNA." She still wasn't convinced, so we asked a few friends who had been actor-directors on other films whether they had run into any particular problems. Diane Ladd, who wrote, directed, and starred in 1995's *Mrs. Munck*, reassured Lisa that it was absolutely doable and gave her tips on how to manage the workload.

Billy Bob Thornton was more succinct. "All the producers

have been telling us this isn't possible," Lisa told him. "They're saying it's too complicated to direct and star in a movie at the same time."

Billy Bob, who wrote, directed, and starred in *Sling Blade*, said, "One word: horseshit."

We took that as a kind of blessing, and with a commitment for financing from Warren Trepp and some money from our own pockets, we were finally off to the races. Lisa wrote, directed, starred in, and coproduced *One Last Dance*, the name we chose for the film. We got an amazing cast of dancers, including my little sister, Bambi, and hired the fantastic George de la Peña to play Nicholas Gunn's role. It's not easy to find people who can both dance and act at the highest level, but George could do both beautifully. He was a former soloist with the American Ballet Theatre and an instinctive, genuine actor. He was perfect for the role.

We shot the film in thirty-two days, mostly in Winnipeg but with a few exteriors shot in New York and LA. I'd had yet another knee surgery just a few weeks before shooting started, so some of the dance scenes were pretty excruciating for me—Lisa had to cut around my grimacing face on more than one occasion. But when all was said and done and Lisa had pulled the footage together, *One Last Dance* was everything we'd hoped it would be. Everyone in the cast and crew had given their hearts and souls to this movie, and it showed.

Seeing the finished film was a culmination of two decades of hard work, dedication, and perseverance, and it was thrilling. *One Last Dance* was released as a DVD and went to number one, and it's still one of the best movies ever made about what it's really like in the world of dance. Lisa showed all the abilities I knew she had, and I loved being directed by her. She had a natural instinct for it, and I was thrilled that she'd finally gotten the chance to put that talent into action.

I'd never been so proud of Lisa, but I was spent by the end of the process. The shooting had been grueling, and there's always a natural letdown when you finish a project you're emotionally invested in. *One Last Dance* was such a deeply personal project that I felt that letdown even more acutely. And before I knew it, I was becoming seriously depressed again.

I don't think I really understood what depression was until this period of my life. I had certainly struggled with deep sadness and feelings of frustration, but my natural optimism had always somehow managed to shine through. In the years following *One Last Dance*, though, that optimism began to desert me entirely. I just couldn't figure out what the point was anymore, and I started drinking again in an effort to numb myself to the creeping feeling of despair. I'd lost the passion and purpose in my life, and couldn't seem to get it back.

I had always felt like a lucky person, but that was being replaced by another feeling: that life wasn't ultimately going to work out the way I'd always thought it would. It felt like this was what real life was—that I was finally growing up and facing the truth, and the truth was ugly. I had first felt it after the horse-riding accident, when I finally realized that no one could simply career through life, completely invincible. For the first forty-six years of my life, I had really believed I was invincible—or had acted as if I was, anyway. When I suddenly realized I wasn't, it was a huge blow. The same thing was now happening emotionally.

Everybody fails in life, but it's when you can't pick yourself up after failure that you're in trouble. I felt like I'd tried to do everything right, but was still getting smacked down. And that made me reluctant to get back up again. Why should I, when the same thing seemed to happen no matter what I did? I hated feeling like the whiny actor—Why can't I be more successful? Why can't I get better roles? But for the first time in my life, I began to fear deep down that I would never bounce back again, that I had no control over my success or failure. And that's a deadly feeling.

As I sank deeper into this hole, and drank more and more, Lisa got to the point where she didn't even recognize me. I had always been resilient, but this person she was living with was beaten down, defeated. Work had always been my cure for feeling depressed, but even that wasn't working anymore.

Lisa was struggling with her own rough patch. Seeing me in pain couldn't help but cause her pain, too. And she also quit smoking during this period, which was about a hundred times harder than she expected, leading to increased feelings of frustration. We were quickly becoming like a couple of rowboats lost in the ocean, looking around for the safety of land but seeing only endless depths ready to swallow us up.

We'd always dealt with whatever issues came up in our relationship. But the biggest issue that cropped up between us in this period was one we couldn't seem to get through. It had to do with a deep temperamental difference between us—the difference between how a Swayze deals with demons and how the rest of the world does.

For years I had been dealing with my demons—feelings of inadequacy, voices trying to undercut me, fears that I was never good enough. The natural instinct is to push them away or ignore them, but the truth is, they always come back. So instead of trying to defeat them, I've tried to use them, to harness that energy rather than denying it. It's a delicate balancing act, trying to toe this line—I went to some very dark places, really struggling with myself, in my efforts to control these negative feelings. And just like all the Swayzes, I never could do anything halfway. When the demons came back worse than ever in this period, I plunged right down into the fray with them.

I found levels of bottom that I didn't even know existed. It wasn't just about drinking, it was about allowing myself to go to these darkest places, allowing myself to feel all the fear and anger and despair that most people spend lifetimes pushing away. Yet as deep as I went, I still felt I was in control. I knew I was dangerously close to the line, but I was choosing to be there.

But for Lisa, this was too much. Seeing me descend into these feelings was scary for her, and my responses to those feelings frightened her, too. There was a lot of anger during this period, and a lot of raw emotion that came out in sudden, jarring spurts. In Lisa's eyes, I was going off the deep end, even though I didn't believe I was. She was afraid one of us would end up dead, and she couldn't take that feeling.

So Lisa made a decision. Without telling me, she packed a couple of suitcases and took off one morning before I woke up. She knew that if she told me she was planning to leave, I would have done anything and everything to try to talk her out of it, including throwing myself in front of the car to keep her from driving off. She didn't want a fight. She felt she had to leave for her own sanity and safety, and she wasn't about to put the matter up for discussion.

When I woke up and found Lisa gone, I was crushed. And

angry. I couldn't believe she'd left me, and I was terrified it would be forever. Lisa and I had been together for more than thirty years by now, and I couldn't bear the thought of life without her. We had made it through so much—how could we lose each other now? I couldn't remember a time in my life when Lisa and I weren't side by side. And I definitely couldn't imagine going forward without her.

Lisa didn't go far, renting an apartment in the San Fernando Valley, about a twenty-minute drive from Rancho Bizarro. She didn't tell anyone she'd moved out, and somehow, miraculously, we managed to keep it a secret from the tabloids and everyone else. We talked every day, and she often came out to the ranch for business. But she was absolutely determined not to come back until things had changed. She kept that apartment for a whole year, which we've never revealed publicly until now.

When Lisa left, I had to completely reevaluate my life. I was driving away the one person who had always stood by me, who had always loved me no matter what. I still didn't know how to change what I was feeling, but there was one thing I could change. I stopped drinking after Lisa moved out, quitting cold turkey for the second time in my life.

The year of our separation was a period of really assessing myself, of learning how to bring myself back from the brink of despair. I was incredibly hurt that Lisa had left, but over time I began to understand that she wasn't doing it to punish me. I began to realize that from her point of view, she'd made it for thirty years, and had gone farther with me into those dark places than most people would have been able to. And that she left only when she felt she had no other choice.

The anger and sense of betrayal I felt at first began to give way to more productive feelings. Rather than spending each day feeling either angry or sorry for myself, I thought about how I could make things better. And how I could win Lisa back.

It was a painful time, but it also taught me all over again how to deal with pain—how I could make it work for me rather than destroy me. Very early on, I had learned how to do that with physical pain. But now I realized that the tools and techniques you use for overcoming physical pain just don't work with emotional pain. Slowly, during this period, I learned the tools and techniques for dealing with emotional pain.

In the midst of our separation, after I'd been sober a few months, I was cast as Allan Quatermain in *King Solomon's Mines*. This was a godsend—a starring role in one of the great heroic narratives in literary history—and it saved my ass. The original *King Solomon's Mines* was a late-nineteenth-century novel about a band of British explorers in Africa, and it had endured as a rollicking adventure tale. I was excited to play this courageous, horse-riding hero, and thrilled to be going back to Africa—a place where both Lisa and I had found such spiritual sustenance during *Steel Dawn*.

In Africa, I was back doing the things I loved best—acting in a period piece, doing stunt work on horseback, spending time in the beauty of nature. I started exploring the African bush, learning again how to live off the land and regaining that feeling of self-worth it always brings. The weeks we spent shooting felt absolutely restorative, as if a slate was being wiped clean. I began to feel again that sense of purpose and passion that I'd lost for so long.

Lisa and I spoke by phone every day, and toward the end of the shoot, she agreed to come to Africa for a visit. I couldn't wait to see her, of course—but as the date drew near, I found myself scared, too. Because it had hurt so badly when she moved out, I subconsciously began protecting myself from the possibility that now she was going to leave me for good. I convinced myself that she was flying all the way to Africa to tell me she wanted a divorce, and braced myself for it.

When Lisa arrived, she felt that I was a little cold to her, and she had no idea why. I didn't think I was being distant, but because I was waiting for her to drop the divorce bomb on me, I most likely was not myself. Ever since her response when I first asked her to marry me all those years ago, I had always feared that deep down, Lisa didn't love me as much as I loved her. Over the decades I had gotten over that feeling, and I had learned to trust her. But when she moved out, it dredged up all those insecurities again, and feelings I had thought were long gone were now as fresh as ever. My excitement at seeing her was buried by my fear.

When a week passed and Lisa didn't ask for a divorce, I was relieved. Maybe she was here just to be with me, after all. So I finally began to let my guard down and enjoy our time together, and when we went for a weeklong safari in Botswana after wrapping, things continued to get better. I was still scared, but as the days went by and we became more comfortable together, I began to dare to believe she might still love me, too.

Yet rifts as deep as the one we'd suffered don't heal overnight. After we returned to California, Lisa moved back home with me, but our troubles weren't over yet. We still weren't really connecting with each other, and the longer that went on, the worse it seemed to get. It was as if we'd made the commitment to make it work, but didn't have the spirit to follow through. Without the necessary nourishment, our relationship was dying a slow death right before our eyes. We wanted to stop it, but we didn't know how.

We ended up in a frustrating pattern: Things would be good for a while, but then we'd go right back into the bad stuff. In Bulgaria, where I was shooting *Icon,* we had the best time we'd had in a while. I said to Lisa, "I'm falling in love with you all over again," and we started talking again about adopting children. We kept thinking we'd turned a corner, but then an argument or angry exchange would plunge us right back down.

After I finished shooting the film *Jump* in Austria, Lisa and I moved to London for seven months, where I performed in *Guys and Dolls* in the West End. During that time, the friction between us grew worse and worse, until it was almost unbearable. We bounced between anger and despair, and our relationship felt poisoned by mistrust and bitterness. After we returned to LA, we had a particularly brutal argument that made it obvious to both of us that things couldn't continue this way.

"I feel like you're torturing me out of this marriage," Lisa said to me, her eyes filled with hurt.

"I feel like you're doing the same thing to me," I replied. We stared at each other for a moment, but there was nothing more to say.

At that point, neither of us knew how to find our way back to the other. But fortunately, we were about to get some assistance—from a very unlikely source.

George de la Peña, who had costarred in *One Last Dance* with us, had become a dear friend since we made the movie. In

2007, for my birthday, he decided to give us a consulting session with a woman he'd written a book with. Elizabeth was a well-known psychic, and George swore by her abilities.

Lisa and I weren't big aficionados of psychic readings, but there was no harm in getting a new perspective on things. I couldn't tell you to this day if she has psychic powers—or if anyone does, really—but the evening she came to Rancho Bizarro, she started picking up on some things very quickly. Maybe George gave her some insight before she came over, or maybe she's just an amazing reader of people and body language. But she cut through the bullshit right away.

We walked with her through the house, showing her each of the rooms so she could get a feel for our life together. As we walked through the dance studio, she stopped short. "There's been entirely too much crying in here," she said. I glanced at Lisa, but she was looking down at the floor. It was true, and we both knew it. The studio, which had once been such a happy place, was permeated with sadness.

We kept walking, and when we ended up in the office in the barn, she said, "Let's sit down right here."

She started talking. She talked about our horses, our furniture, the feng shui of our home. And then, suddenly, she looked straight at Lisa. "There's something really weird happening," she said. "You're sitting right there, but it's like you're not really here."

Lisa just stared at her. "Yes. You're here, but you're not really," she went on. "It's like you've checked out already." And Lisa burst into tears.

Elizabeth turned to me. "She's already gone," she said. "You need to really look at what she wants, at how to fix this. Because she is out the door."

I looked at Lisa, whose face was streaked with tears. "She's right," Lisa said. "In my heart, I'm gone. I'm gone."

I felt the tears well up, too. What was Lisa saying? Had I really lost her for good? Was it too late to do anything?

"What do you want, Lisa?" I asked her. "What can I do?" She sobbed quietly beside me, and my heart just about broke open. I wanted to grab her, to hold her and never let her go, but all I could do was touch her shoulder gently and look her in the eyes.

And then a strange and wonderful thing happened. We looked at each other, and somehow we each suddenly saw once again the person we'd fallen in love with. I hadn't been able to see that for so long, since we had so many layers of pain that had built up over the years. But in that one moment, instead of seeing someone we'd fought with, or felt angry toward, or resented, all of that simply fell away. I felt a surge of love for Lisa that I hadn't felt in years. I took her into my arms and we cried together, our tears washing away the pain that had been keeping us so far apart.

We started talking, really talking, like we hadn't done in years. When two people are at odds, sometimes the hardest thing to do is decide who will step through the door first to try to repair things. Too often, one person is ready to go but the other isn't. But with the help of Elizabeth, Lisa and I came together again. We both opened our hearts at the same time, reaching toward each other in a way we'd all but forgotten. And at her suggestion, we each wrote "I will forget the past" ten times on a piece of paper, then buried those papers under an avocado tree in our yard. It was time for a fresh start.

People always ask us, How do we do it? How have we kept a marriage of thirty-four years and counting so strong? I don't claim to have any great answers, but I do know one thing. Lisa and I never, ever stopped trying, no matter how bad things got. We never gave up on each other, although in our absolute worst moments, we came very close. If there was a way to save our relationship, we were going to find it. And the very fact that we both always wanted to save it meant that there was a way to do it. Because that desire is the key. As I said to Lisa not long after our experience with Elizabeth, just as an argument was starting to break out, "We're stopping this right now. I never want to go back to the way it was."

Our experience with Elizabeth was definitely life-changing. But the funny thing was, the next time we saw her after that, she got just about everything wrong—go figure. We have talked to her since then, and she amazed us once again with great insights and advice. But the only thing that really matters to us is that she helped us come together in a moment when we were both open to it. And we took it from there.

With our relationship back on track, we were ready and eager to face the world again. I'll always be grateful that we were, because the next twist that came was the cruelest of all.

# Chapter 15

With so few good movie roles available, I'd been looking off and on for a TV series over the past couple of years—but though I'd read tons of scripts, nothing was ever quite right. I had really enjoyed working on *The Renegades* and *North and South*, and knew if I could find a good character on a solid series it would be worth gunning for. Then, in 2007, my long-time agent, Nicole David, and manager for TV Jenny Delaney sent me scripts for two new series that both looked very good.

One of the two shows, *The Beast*, was about an enigmatic FBI agent named Charles Barker. Barker was a fascinating, layered character who constantly surprised me as I read through the script. I loved his world-weary persona, and the fact that he wasn't your stereotypical good guy, but a complex and mature character.

I really liked the writing and the ideas on *The Beast*, but the production team was young and inexperienced, especially compared to the team for the other series. Going with the young, hungry show would be a risk, but ultimately I just liked the material better. There was something about Barker that really spoke to me, so in the end I turned the other project down.

We shot the pilot, and I knew even before seeing the finished product that *The Beast* was going to be really good. If it got picked up, we'd be shooting the full first season in Chicago, and both Lisa and I had high hopes that would be the case. So we went into the holiday period more optimistic than we had been in a long while—happy to be in love and excited about the future.

Then came that fateful night in Aspen. As we toasted the new year and I felt the champagne burn my stomach, I never could have guessed what lay ahead. I didn't think my digestive issues and that strange burning sensation meant anything serious, even though I noticed that I had begun losing some weight, too. But I just gritted my teeth and made it through the holidays, assuming I'd start feeling better soon.

Back in LA a couple of weeks later, I noticed something else strange. When I went to the bathroom, which had become something of an ordeal over the past few weeks with all my digestive issues, things didn't look quite right. It's embarrassing to say, but my urine was very dark, and my stool was very pale. I walked out to the kitchen and found Lisa making a cup of tea. "Something really weird is going on," I said, and told her what I'd noticed. She knew I hadn't been feeling all that great, and she asked if anything else wasn't quite right.

I walked to a mirror and peered at my face. "Do my eyes look yellow?" I asked Lisa. She came to look, and I pulled my lower lids down and rolled my eyes around.

"Yes," she said. "They do. They look jaundiced." Lisa's not the worrying kind, but I could tell by the look on her face that she was concerned. "Let's make an appointment for you to see Dr. Davidson tomorrow," she said.

"I don't think that's really necessary," I said. "I'm sure it'll clear up."

But Lisa was adamant. "This isn't normal," she said. So we made an appointment, then got online to see what we could find out about these strange symptoms I was having. We looked up jaundice and found a long list of things that could cause it, none of which sounded very good—from hepatitis to liver infection to cancer. All the same, we didn't imagine for a second that I could possibly be that sick.

The next day, January 14, Lisa and I went to Cedars-Sinai to see Dr. Davidson. We described my symptoms, and after looking at my eyes he immediately ordered a batch of tests. CAT scans, blood tests, urine test—they put me through the works. He knew something was up, and a procedure called a bilirubin test soon confirmed it. My bilirubin levels were very high, which meant something strange was going on with my bile ducts.

We asked what might be the cause of high bilirubin levels, and he gave us a short list of possibilities, one of which was pancreatic cancer. But another was acute pancreatitis, which is still a serious illness, but treatable. "It's probably pancreatitis," I told Lisa, trying to reassure not only her but myself, too.

But later that day, a CAT scan revealed a mass on my pancreas. This was very bad news, though it still didn't mean I definitely had cancer. To find out for sure, the doctors would need to do an exploratory endoscopic procedure, to get a piece of tissue for testing. Unfortunately, they couldn't schedule the endoscopy until four days later—an eternity when you're dealing with a fast-moving disease. We spent the next four days at home in a fog, trying to keep our emotions in check while inside we were starting to panic.

The endoscopy was scheduled for January 19. An anesthesiologist put me to sleep, and a gastrointestinal surgeon snaked a tube down my throat. He planned to insert a stent into my bile duct, to open it up and have a better look. But he couldn't get the scope that far down, because my stomach was very enlarged. They would have to try again another time, using a different technique—but at this point, they were almost certain what was wrong with me. There were very few things other than pancreatic cancer that would cause my stomach to swell like that along with the other symptoms.

As I lay sleeping off the anesthesia in the recovery room, two of the doctors gave Lisa the news. "We need to do a pathology on the tissue to be absolutely certain," they told her, "but we're 99 percent sure that he's got pancreatic cancer."

Lisa later told me she went completely numb hearing those words. She didn't trust herself to absorb any more information these doctors were giving her, but she knew it was critically important, so she managed to ask them to call her sister-in-law Maria Scoures. Maria is a respected oncologist in Houston, and Lisa needed her help to take in this news and help decide what to do next. The doctors got Maria on the phone, and she's been a godsend for us both from that moment on.

Lying in the recovery room, I still had no idea what awaited me. When I woke up, I was suffering from severe enough cramps that the doctors ordered me to spend the night in the hospital. During the endoscopy, the doctors had pumped me full of air while trying to get the stent in, and having all that air trapped in my digestive system was unbelievably painful. They wheeled me into a hospital room and I tried to make myself comfortable, still groggy from the anesthesia.

Lisa came in to see me, but first she made a decision: She wouldn't tell me about the cancer right away. She wanted me to have one last night of "normal" life—one last night of innocence before our hardest fight began. She told me she loved me, and spent the night by my side.

The next morning, the surgeon came in and woke us both up to give me the diagnosis. I don't remember much about that conversation, but when he told me I had pancreatic cancer, my first thought was, "I'm a dead man." The only thing I'd ever heard about pancreatic cancer was that it's incurable and it kills you very quickly. I just stared at him in shock. I had gone in for a simple gastrointestinal procedure, then all of a sudden—surprise! You could be dead before springtime!

Fear sliced through me. What the fuck had just happened? I had been so excited about the upswing my life was on. Now it all seemed like a cruel joke. I couldn't be dying—I had too much to live for! I just couldn't face the idea that life as I'd always known it was over, that there was a disease inside me that would grow and mutate and eventually kill me. I didn't know where I would find the strength to deal with it.

And neither did Lisa. She has always been so strong, so determined and capable. We had been together through so much. But after the surgeon left, she just broke down and cried. She crawled into the hospital bed with me, buried her head in my neck, and said, "I can't do this, Buddy. I can't do it. You can ask me for anything else, but please don't ask me to do this." I held her tightly and we wept together. She knew I couldn't change anything about what was happening, but she was devastated.

She pulled herself together and has helped me through every aspect of this disease with good humor and boundless love. But at that moment, as she lay sobbing in my arms, I felt as alone as I'd ever felt. I knew I'd have to find a way to fight this thing, but the very thought of it exhausted me.

There was one last sliver of hope. If the cancer hadn't spread at all, the doctors told us it might be possible to operate. But that hope came crashing down the next day, when another CAT scan showed that it had already spread to my liver. I had what they call Stage 4 cancer, the worst possible.

Lisa and I decided to tell only a few people about my diagnosis, at least until we knew for sure what my treatment would be and what my prognosis really was. We told our lawyer Fred Gaines, agent Nicole David, and my brother Donny. We especially didn't want to tell my mother, as she was having eye surgery the next day and was supposed to try to keep her eyes dry—no crying—for a few weeks after the surgery.

Unfortunately, those morally bankrupt souls at the *National Enquirer* had other ideas. Someone in the medical field tipped them off, and a *National Enquirer* reporter showed up at my mom's house about a week after my diagnosis. She opened the door to have a complete stranger ask, "How do you feel about Patrick having pancreatic cancer?" And that's how she found out. For the life of me, I cannot understand how anyone can be so cruel, so unfeeling, to do such a thing. But human decency is apparently an afterthought when there's money to be made selling tabloids.

Lisa and I jumped right into action, learning everything we

possibly could about the disease and how to treat it. Maria was a tremendous help, too—she was doing pancreatic cancer research of her own, and advised us on how best to fight it. From the beginning, we've done all our own home care—injections, intravenous nutrition, and everything else—because we didn't want to have an at-home nurse. We wanted life to go on as normally as it possibly could, because I had no intention of staying alive just for the sake of it—I wanted to live and enjoy life rather than feeling like a full-time patient.

Before the news of my illness broke publicly, the A&E network decided to pick up *The Beast* for a full season. This was incredibly great news—but of course, they'd ordered those thirteen episodes without knowing their lead actor had just been diagnosed with pancreatic cancer. At first, I wasn't sure I could go through with filming a full season of an action-packed dramatic series—I didn't know whether I'd be healthy enough to do it. But very soon, I realized there was nothing I wanted to do more. And I made up my mind that I'd find a way, no matter what.

We got in touch with A&E to let them know about my diagnosis, and I sent along this message: "Don't count me out. I can do this." All I could think was, if I'm really going out, I'd rather go out on a high note, doing quality work I believe in. I loved *The Beast,* and felt that I'd done some of the best work of my career in the pilot. I really wanted to have the chance to explore the character of Charles Barker even further.

Once they learned about the cancer, the executives at A&E were under no obligation to keep their offer on the table. It would have been the easiest thing in the world for them to kill the series. But to their immense credit, they did not. We decided to see how my chemotherapy treatment went, and they'd make a decision after that. If I responded well and it looked as if I'd be healthy enough to shoot the series, they'd go ahead with it.

Television executives aren't necessarily renowned for their generosity of spirit, but that decision by A&E president Bob DiBitetto restored my faith in humanity. It was such a decent, openhearted thing to do—and he kept his word. After a few months of chemotherapy treatment, when I was feeling pretty good, I invited the writers and producers to Rancho Bizarro. I told them I was excited to do the series and ready to go, and they called A&E right then to ask for the green light. We got it.

Chemotherapy was hell on wheels, and it got worse the longer it went on—but I knew if it was a matter of just pushing through all the pain and discomfort, I could do it. The cancer also caused all kinds of trouble with my digestive system, including bloody, painful bowel movements and debilitating cramps. I spent many nights curled up in the fetal position on the bathroom floor, desperate for the pain to pass. But although I felt nauseated, bloated, and cramped most of the time, there was at least one side effect of chemo I'd dreaded but didn't suffer: I managed to keep my hair.

As Lisa and I headed up to Chicago to begin shooting in the late summer of 2008, I vowed to myself that no one on the set would ever know if I was feeling bad or in pain. I was going to shoot this whole series, doing my own stunts, right into the Chicago winter—and I wasn't going to make a peep about anything having to do with cancer or treatment. If I had a 6:30 A.M. call, I'd wake up a couple of hours earlier to try to get my digestive system in order and make sure I was ready to go.

I stayed on that first chemo regimen for ten months, which is an incredibly long time—most people undergo a round of chemo for just a few months, as the side effects get cumulatively worse. And mine did get worse toward the end of shooting the season, but I undertook an attitude adjustment every single day, reminding myself how fortunate I was to be working on a project I loved, and willing myself to put one foot in front of the other to finish it, no matter how bad I felt.

Being on the set was incredibly energizing. I was happy to be working again, focusing on something other than the continuing fight against cancer. I worked twelve- to eighteen-hour days, jumping and fighting my way through action sequences and thoroughly enjoying bringing Charles Barker to life. There were definitely tough moments when I had to overcome pain, nausea, and fatigue. But some days were good. Once, after a crew member said to me, "I can't believe you're able to do all this," I turned to Lisa and said, "I've worked with hangovers worse than this."

I continued with chemotherapy all the way through the shoot, but I never took any painkillers, since they dull not only your pain but also your sharpness. If I was going to do great work on this series, I wanted to be 100 percent there. And if that meant dealing with extra pain, that was the price that had to be paid. By the ninth episode, I didn't know if I could finish, as the bad days were really, really bad. I was upset with myself, angry and embarrassed that I might have overestimated my ability to push through. But quitting was not an option. I dug deeper—far deeper than I ever had—and pushed through to finish the season. In five months of shooting, I missed only a day and a half of work, and that was because of the sniffles.

I didn't take on this challenge in order to become an inspiration to other cancer patients. But when reports came out that I was starting to shoot a new TV series, a full six months after being diagnosed with an illness that kills most people within weeks, we started receiving all kinds of letters and cards from people who found it inspiring. I'm grateful for the huge response from people, but really I just wanted to make a great TV show.

As always, Lisa was an equal partner in creating and honing the character I played. She spent the whole shoot in Chicago, and she also directed one of the thirteen episodes. Working with her again, and watching her craft what became a fantastic episode, was amazingly gratifying. We were in this together, in every possible way—just as we had always been.

It's a fact that Swayze men have never lived to ripe old ages. My father died at age fifty-seven, the same age I am now. My paternal grandfather also died young, and most of my uncles never saw the other side of forty.

In some ways, I've always felt as if I was living on borrowed time. I've cheated death more times than I can count, from motorcycle accidents to horse accidents to the airplane incident to teetering on a ledge with David Carradine. There's something in the Swayze makeup that loves risk, and God knows I've embraced my share over the years. After I passed the age of thirty with my body and mind still intact, I always felt I'd gotten away with something.

The months I've spent fighting this cancer have been an emotional roller coaster. There are days when I feel determined to live until a cure is found, and truly believe I can do it. And there are days when I'm so tired, I just don't know how

I can keep on going. But I have to. I have to keep moving forward as if there's a long future for me. As if this is beatable. I'm not running around like some kind of Pollyanna—it's more of a dead-set, clenched-jaw determination. I'll just be damned if this son of a bitch is going to beat me. It's trying to kill me, but I'm going to return the favor.

In all my life, I never gave up in a fight, starting from that day in junior high when five boys were whaling on me at once. And I'm not going to give up now.

I have so much to live for. So much I want to accomplish, so many things I want to explore. Since we've had our ranch in New Mexico, Lisa and I have been working on conservation and preservation of the land. We commissioned a two-hundred-year forest-stewardship plan that not only would maintain forest growth levels, but also improve them. Lisa and I are passionate about being good stewards of this beautiful land, and we want to share the knowledge we've gained with others, to help spread the word about conservation.

When we bought our ranch in New Mexico, it was the fulfillment of a lifelong dream. I swore when my dad died that I would one day own a ranch and return to my cowboy roots. I also swore I'd do everything I could to make him proud for the rest of my life. There's no better way to do both those things than by keeping this land pristine and beautiful for generations to come. I am my father's son, and I'm living the life he dreamed of having. In every way imaginable, it's worth living for.

There's also so much more I want to accomplish as an artist. I've been writing new music in the last few months, and am always looking at potential roles that come up. I still have the energy and the drive to take on new projects, and have no patience for anyone who suggests otherwise. Whenever someone asks me what I think my legacy is, I say the same thing: I'm not finished yet! My work is my legacy, and there's a whole lot more I have to give.

And of course, there's my relationship with Lisa. I can't even begin to express what she has meant to me over the years. As a naïve and insecure twenty-year-old, I would never have dreamed that one person could find so much passion and so much loyalty with another. Lisa and I are a part of each other— I can no more imagine life without her than I can imagine living without my own heart. And feeling that love for her is that much sweeter after the hard times we went through.

In the summer of 2008, just before we went to Chicago to film *The Beast,* Lisa and I decided on the spur of the moment to renew the vows we'd made to each other thirty-three years before. We put the whole thing together in four days, and invited a handful of close friends and family members to join us. I rode in on a white stallion, and together Lisa and I stood hand in hand and recited the vows we'd each written. As she finished saying the words she'd written for me, tears came to my eyes.

> While the future is an unknown, the one thing I do know is that I will love you. I'm very lucky to have found you in my life and am grateful that I have had the ability to open my eyes and see just what I have. . . .
>
> Because what I have—the love, the greatness and enormity of what I feel, informs everything around me, and brings me back to what I cherish most. And in cherishing the most there is for me, I cherish you more.

And then I spoke the words I'd written for her.

How do I tell you how lucky I feel, that you fell into my life? How grateful I am that you chose to love me? I know that because of you, I found my spirit, I saw the man I wanted to be. But most of all, you were my friend.

Together, we've created journeys that were beyond anything we could imagine. Journeys that dreams are made of. We have ridden into the sunset on a white stallion, countless times. We've tasted the dust in the birthplaces of religions. Yet you still take my breath away. I'm still not complete until I look in your eyes.

You are my woman, my lover, my mate and my lady. I've loved you forever, I love you now and I will love you forevermore.

Even with everything we've been through, and everything we still are facing, it was one of the happiest days of my life. And it made me more determined than ever to have as many more beautiful days together with her as I possibly can.

# Acknowledgments

We'd like to thank our families for all their love and support: Ed and Maria, Eric and Mary, Paul and Jessica, John, Alex and Carol, Sean and Jami, Bambi and Don—and especially our mothers, Patsy Swayze and Karin Niemi, who entrusted us with their treasured photos and memories. And we're grateful to my brother Donny Swayze for his great memory, and for really being there for us as I've battled cancer over the last year and a half.

It took a lot of work to bring this book together, and it wouldn't be what it is without the help of Lisa Dickey. Her focus, suggestions, and skill at helping shape a story are fantastic. She is a joy to work with, and we'd work with her again in a heartbeat. Jessica Haapaniemi spent countless hours helping with transcriptions, research, and photos. Our literary agent, Mel Berger, is a wonderful counselor and true gentleman and has been there for us anytime we've needed him. And Mel's assistant, Graham, is always upbeat and helpful.

Our editor at Atria, Sarah Durand, believed in this project from the start and shepherded it with care. We're grateful for her hard work and skill, and also want to thank her colleague,

Sarah Cantin, who provided tremendous support. And our good friend, Lynne Butler, was a great sounding board and gave us excellent feedback.

We've been lucky enough to work with an amazing group of people for more than twenty-five years now. We call them "The Team"—real professionals who are also real friends. Annett Wolf, of WKT Public Relations, has been with us through thick and thin. In addition to being a phenomenal publicist, she has given us wonderful and astute guidance in telling our story, and her assistant Jayme Phillips helped tremendously with our photos. Fred Gaines, our lawyer extraordinaire, has also been looking out for us for more than twenty-five years—and being a literary nut himself, he gave us great feedback in addition to invaluable legal advice. Our fabulous agent, Nicole David, was one of the first to suggest we do this book. She's the best agent anyone could ever hope for, and she and TV manager Jenny Delaney have not only helped to shape our careers, they've always stood strong beside us.

Throughout the years, we've been incredibly fortunate to work with the most talented people in the worlds of film, television, dance, and theater. We've also been blessed with an amazing group of friends, who've given us unlimited love and support. It would take another whole book to thank everyone by name, but to all those who've been there for us—you know who you are—we thank you from the bottom of our hearts. We'd also like to thank the fantastic doctors who have spearheaded my care and treatment, and helped me stay healthy enough to do this book—George Fisher, David Hoffman, Maria Scouros, and Mary Mulcahy.

And finally, a big thank-you to our fans: for buying movie tickets; watching our work on film, TV, and stage; and listening to the music all these years. Not only have you made my career possible, but your heartfelt wishes and support this past year and a half have helped to arm us in this battle against cancer. It's amazing how much inspiration and drive to keep fighting we've drawn from everyone's letters and prayers. Thanks to you all; we hope to be giving you much more to see and hear in the years to come.